SIMPLE CHIC *Knits*

KAREN MILLER AND SUSAN RITCHIE

OF MRS MOON

CICO BOOKS

LONDON NEW YORK

For Dad, who would have been so proud.

Published in 2016 by CICO Books
An imprint of Ryland Peters & Small Ltd
20–21 Jockey's Fields, London WC1R 4BW
341 E116th St, New York, NY 10029

www.rylandpeters.com

10 9 8 7 6 5 4 3 2 1

A CIP catalog record for this book is
available from the Library of Congress
and the British Library.

ISBN: 978-1-78249-310-5

Printed in China

Editor: Kate Haxell
Designer: Vicky Rankin
Photographers: Penny Wincer and Emma Mitchell
Stylists: Nel Haynes and Rob Merrett
Illustrator: Stephen Dew

Art director: Sally Powell
Production manager: Gordana Simakovic
Publishing manager: Penny Craig
Publisher: Cindy Richards

SIMPLE CHIC *Knits*

Contents

Introduction 6

Introduction

It has been so lovely to have the opportunity to write a book that indulges our passion for beautiful knitwear. Whenever we design something it is always with a view to wearing it or using it ourselves, so our love of a relaxed, classic but contemporary style comes through loud and clear in *Simple Chic Knits*—and we hope that you enjoy sharing our outlook!

When we opened our yarn store, Mrs Moon, in London back in 2009, we had a vision of a beautiful space full of color, old-fashioned values, and casually classy style. We like to think we managed to achieve that, and as Mrs Moon has changed from retailer to designer and manufacturer of our own gorgeous yarn, Plump, our initial vision has not changed. We love color and we love simplicity—in busy lives less is always more!

In this book we have created a range of designs that anyone can have a go at. They are all simple: some very simple, others quite simple, but none of the techniques are beyond a new knitter who is prepared to put in a bit of practice. From page 106 onward you'll find step-by-step illustrations for the techniques used in the projects—from casting on to making loops—and, with the wonderful age of the Internet, there is always someone out there who has filmed a technique for you (including us at www.mrsmoon.co.uk), if you find videos easier to follow.

We have always designed garments, accessories, and homewares that we not only want for ourselves, but also don't begrudge knitting. So nothing is too big or too tricky. We obviously have quite short attention spans, so you'll find that everything can be finished quickly—some projects can literally be done in an evening, others might take a week, but nothing should take months, because where's the fun in that?

We have been lucky enough to be able to use some of the most luxurious natural fibers and we would encourage you to find the best yarns you can for your lovingly made projects. But if you can't find the exact yarn we used, or can't justify the cost, then please don't be put off. All the projects include the standard gauge (tension) of the yarns used so you can easily substitute any of them—your local yarn store is a great place to start, and it needs your support!

We've had such fun designing and creating these simple, chic knits, and we hope you'll enjoy making them, too.

Karen and Susan xx

CHAPTER 1

For the Home

The homewares in this chapter are great projects to try if you have mastered the basic knitted fabrics and now want to explore some creative patterns and textures. As there isn't any shaping to deal with in the pillows, blanket, runner, and hot water bottle cozy, you can concentrate on getting the stitch patterns perfect. The Zig-Zag Blanket (see page 18) is probably the most time-consuming project in the whole book, but it's a very simple technique and repeat pattern, so it's not difficult to knit.

CLUSTER STITCH *Pillow*

The great thing about a knitted pillow is that it can add fabulous texture as well as color to a room. Choosing a chunky yarn that is very quick to knit up means that you can add to your room's look in an afternoon.

To do the clusters you knit a group of six stitches onto a double-pointed needle, wind the yarn around them, then slide them off the other end of the needle. You do need a double-pointed needle that is the same size as your knitting needles—rather than a cable needle—to ensure that the stitches are the correct size.

Yarn
Mrs Moon Plump (80% superfine merino wool, 20% baby alpaca) super-bulky (super-chunky) yarn, 3½oz (100g), 76yd (70m) skeins
  2 skeins in Gooseberry Fool
  2 skeins in same or contrast color for back (optional: I used Damson Jam)

Other materials
16in (40cm) square pillow pad
17in (42cm) square of fabric for pillow back (optional)

Needles and equipment
1 pair of US 15 (10mm) straight knitting needles
1 US 15 (10mm) double-pointed needle
Large-eyed knitter's sewing needle

Size
16 x 16in (40 x 40cm)

Gauge (tension)
Project gauge (tension) is 10 sts and 10 rows to 4in (10cm) over st st using US 15 (10mm) needles.
Standard ball band gauge (tension) is 10 sts and 10 rows to 4in (10cm) over st st using US 15 (10mm) needles.

Abbreviations
See page 126.
CL6 = cluster 6: see page 121 for step-by-step illustrations.

PILLOW FRONT
Using US 15 (10mm) needles, cast on 42 sts.
Row 1 (RS): P2, [k2, p2] to end.
Row 2 and all even-numbered rows: K2, [p2, k2] to end.
Row 3: P2, [CL6, p2] to end.
Row 4: As row 2.
Row 5: As row 1.
Row 6: As row 2.
Row 7: P2, k2, p2, [CL6, p2] to last 4 sts, k2, p2.
Row 8: As row 2.
Rep rows 1–8, 5 more times, then rep rows 1–4 once more.
Bind (cast) off in k2, p2 rib patt.

At this stage, the pillow front looks much longer and narrower than your pillow pad but have faith (!), once stretched across the pad it should fit perfectly.

PILLOW BACK

You can repeat the front design if you would like. Alternatively, cast on 42 stitches using a contrast color and knit in st st until the work measures 16½in (41cm), then bind (cast) off.

TO MAKE UP

Weave in ends (see page 124).
First, neatly sew the top and bottom edges together. You will need to stretch the front piece across the back to make them the same width, so pin it first to make sure that you stretch it evenly, and use backstitch (see page 124) to sew up. Once these two seams are done, backstitch one side seam before stuffing the pillow pad in. Sew the last side seam using mattress stitch (see page 125).

HERRINGBONE *Bed Runner*

I love herringbone stitch; it's a real show stopper, but also easy to get to grips
with. If you've never done this stitch before, I would have a little practice
before you start your runner. Herringbone stitch is fiendishly difficult to unpick
if you make a mistake, so working a few short rows to get the hang of it is
well worth the effort!

There are three different sizes given for this runner, so choose the one that best
fits your bed.

Yarn
Mrs Moon Plump (80% superfine merino wool,
20% baby alpaca) super-bulky (super-chunky) yarn,
3½oz (100g), 76yd (70m) skeins
    2(2:2) skeins in Rhubarb Crumble (A)
    2(2:2) skeins in Fondant Fancy (B)
    1(2:2) skeins in Clotted Cream (C)
    1(2:2) skeins in Pistachio Ice Cream (D)
    1(2:2) skeins in Peppermint Cream (E)

Needles and equipment
US 35 (20mm) circular needle, at least 32in (80cm) long
Large-eyed knitter's sewing needle

Size
Approx. 50(63:67¼) x 23in (128(160:171) x 59cm)

Gauge (tension)
Project gauge (tension) is 9 sts and 8 rows to 4in (10cm)
over herringbone patt using US 15 (10mm) needles.
Standard ball band gauge (tension) is 10 sts and
10 rows to 4in (10cm) over st st using US 15
(10mm) needles.

Abbreviations
See page 126.

HOW TO WORK
HERRINGBONE STITCH

For herringbone, each stitch—apart from the very first one in the row—is worked twice. The wrong-side rows are quite simple, but on the right-side rows the stitches are twisted before you knit them, which slows the process down. You twist the right-side row stitches using ssk (slip, slip, knit: see page 116), but only twist each stitch the first time you work it. This might sound a little complicated, but if you pick up needles and yarn and follow the instructions, it will make sense.

You start this runner with a wrong-side row, so those instructions are given first.

WRONG-SIDE ROW

Purl the first two stitches on the left-hand needle together, but only slip the first stitch off the left-hand needle. *Now, purl together the next two stitches—the stitch that has already been worked but left on the left-hand needle, and the next stitch—and again, just slip the first one off the left-hand needle. Rep from * until you have just one stitch left on the left-hand needle, then purl this stitch.

RIGHT-SIDE ROW

Slip the first stitch on the left-hand needle knitwise onto the right-hand needle, then slip the second stitch knitwise onto the right-hand needle. Insert the left-hand needle into the front of these two stitches and knit them together, but only slip the first stitch off the left-hand needle. *Now, put the right-hand needle into the front of the first stitch on the left-hand needle and slip it onto the right-hand needle, slip the second stitch knitwise onto the right-hand needle, insert the the left-hand needle into the front of these two stitches, and knit them together, but only slip the first stitch off the left-hand needle. Rep from * until you have just one stitch left on the left-hand needle, then knit this stitch.

BED RUNNER

Using A, cast on 116(144:154) sts loosely.

Starting with a WS row, work in herringbone stitch (see left), changing colors as folls:

Rows 1–2: A.
Rows 3–4: B.
Rows 5–6: C.
Rows 7–8: D.
Rows 9–11: E.
Rows 12–13: D.
Rows 14–15: C.
Rows 16–17: B.
Row 18: A.

Rep these 18 rows once more, then rep rows 1–2 once more (38 rows in total). Bind (cast) off loosely.

TO MAKE UP

Weave in ends (see page 124).

SWEETIE *Bolster*

Reminiscent of an old-fashioned wrapped candy or sweetie, this bolster cover is simple to fit onto what can be a rather tricky shape. A series of holes is created at either end to thread ribbon through and gather the ends up. You can choose a contrast ribbon or yarn tie, or if you prefer you can use the yarn that you knitted with and so keep the tie out of sight.

Yarn

Debbie Bliss Rialto Chunky (100% extra fine merino) bulky (chunky) yarn, 1¾oz (50g), 65yd (60m) balls
    7 balls in Silver

Other materials

2yd (2m) of ⅝in (15mm) double-faced satin ribbon, or another desired ribbon or yarn
Bolster pillow pad measuring 18 x 6¾in diameter (45 x 17cm diameter)

Needles and equipment

1 pair of US 10½ (6.5mm) straight knitting needles
Cable needle
Large-eyed knitter's sewing needle

Size

Knitted piece is 31 x 20in (79 x 53cm) (when stretched)

Gauge (tension)

Project gauge (tension) is 15 sts and 21 rows to 4in (10cm) over st st using US 10½ (6.5mm) needles.
Standard ball band gauge (tension) is 15 sts and 21 rows to 4in (10cm) over st st using US 10½ (6.5mm) needles.

Abbreviations

See page 126.
C8B = cable 8 back: see page 120 for step-by-step illustrations.

BOLSTER COVER

Using US 10½ (6.5mm) needles, cast on 84 sts.
Row 1: [K1, p1] to end.
Row 1 sets the rib patt.
Rep row 1, 13 more times or until work measures 3½in (8.5cm).
Next row (eyelets): K3, [yo, k2tog, k2] to last 5 sts, yo, k2tog, k3.
Next row: Purl.
Cont in st st for 14 rows or until work measures 6¾in (17cm) from cast on edge, ending with a WS row.

START CABLE PATT
Row 1 (RS): K4, [p2, k8, p2, k4] to end.
Row 2 and all even-numbered rows: P4, [k2, p8, k2, p4] to end.
Row 3: K4, [p2, C8B, p2, k4] to end.
Row 4: As row 2.
Rep rows 1–2, 3 more times. (*10 rows completed*)
These 10 rows set the cable patt.
Rep the patt 7 more times, then rep rows 1–3 once more.

Next row (WS): Purl.
Next row: Knit.
Cont in st st for 13 more rows.
Next row (RS): K3, [yo, k2tog, k2]
to last 5 sts, yo, k2tog, k3.
Next row: [K1, p1] to end.
Rep last row 13 more times or until
rib measures 3½in (8.5cm).
Bind (cast) off in patt.

TO MAKE UP

Weave in ends (see page 124).
Using mattress stitch (see page 125),
or backstitch (see page 124) with
right sides facing, sew up the long
seam. Turn the cover right side out.
Cut ribbon in half and weave
one length in and out of the holes.
Tie tightly and then tie a bow to
finish off. Repeat at the other end.

WORKING CABLES

Every cable simply involves moving a group of stitches off the
left-hand needle and working the next group on that needle first,
followed by the ones you've moved. You hold the stitches at either
the front or the back of your knitting while you knit the next group,
so cables are either called F (front) or B (back) accordingly; (see
page 120 for step-by-step instructions). Any good knitting pattern
will tell you how the cable should work, so you don't need to
memorize every combination or permutation to cable routinely!
One thing to know is that in a written cable instruction—in this
instance C8B—the 8 refers to the total number of stitches involved
in the cable. You are generally only moving half of these stitches
onto the cable needle.
Also, don't be too concerned about having an "official" cable
needle; I don't have any. Pencils come in handy (as long as they
are thinner than the needle you are using), but I mostly use any
double-pointed needle that happens to be lying around: much
more useful in the long run.

ZIG-ZAG *Blanket*

This funky zig-zag blanket would be great for any sofa, or for a special baby's crib. You can tailor the colors according to your taste, but I love mixing vibrant shades to create something amazing.

The pattern is a simple slipstitch that is reversed along the row, and then also reversed at the center of the blanket to create a concentric diamond pattern.

You need to concentrate, but the technique itself is very simple as you are only ever handling one color of yarn at a time, and you don't have to strand the color not in use across the back of the knitting.

Yarn

Mrs Moon Plump DK (80% superfine merino wool, 20% baby alpaca) light-worsted-weight (double knitting) yarn, 1¾oz (50g), 125yd (115m) skeins

   2 skeins in Clotted Cream (A)
   4 skeins in Gooseberry Fool (B)
   4 skeins in Rhubarb Crumble (C)

Needles and equipment

US 6 (4mm) 32in (80cm) circular needle
US 7 (4.5mm) 32in (80cm) circular needle
2 stitch markers (or scraps of yarn)
Large-eyed knitter's sewing needle

Size

26¾ x 35in (68 x 89cm) (blocked)

Gauge (tension)

Project gauge (tension) is 24 sts and 40 rows to 4in (10cm) over zigzag patt using US 7 (4.5mm) needles.
Standard ball band gauge (tension) is 20–22 sts and 30 rows to 4in (10cm) over st st using US 6–7 (4–4.5mm) needles.

Abbreviations

See page 126.
Note that all stitches are slipped purlwise (see page 113).

BLANKET

BOTTOM BORDER
Using US 6 (4mm) needle and A, cast on 201 sts.
Row 1 (WS): [K1, p1] to last st, k1.
Row 1 sets the seed (moss) border patt.
Rep the patt 7 more times
Change to US 7 (4.5mm) needle and B.
Row 9: Purl, placing a marker after the 100th and 101st stitches.

These 8 rows form the zig-zag patt.
Rep patt 14 more times, then rep rows 1–4 once more.

REVERSED ZIG-ZAG PATT
Row 1 (RS): Using C, k4, [sl1, k3] to marker, sm, sl1, sm, [k3, sl1] to last 4 sts, k4.
Row 2: Using C, p4, [sl1, p3] to marker, sm, sl1, sm, [p3, sl1] to last 4 sts, p4.
Row 3: Using B, [k3, sl1] to marker, sm, k1, sm, [sl1, k3] to end.
Row 4: Using B, [p3, sl1] to marker, sm, p1, sm, [sl1, p3] to end.
Row 5: Using C, k2, [sl1, k3] to last 3 sts, (slipping markers), sl1, k2.
Row 6: Using C, p2, [sl1, p3] to last 3 sts, (slipping markers), sl1, p2.
Row 7: Using B, k1, [sl1, k3] to 3 sts before marker, sl1, k5 (slipping markers), [sl1, k3] to last 2 sts, sl1, k1.
Row 8: Using B, p1, [sl1, p3] to 3 sts before marker, sl1, p5, (slipping markers), [sl1, p3] to last 2 sts, sl1, p1.
These 8 rows form the reversed zig-zag patt.
Rep patt 14 more times, then rep rows 1–2 once more.
Using A, knit one row, removing markers.

TOP BORDER
Change to US 6 (4mm) needle.
Next row: [K1, p1] to last st, k1.
Last row sets the seed (moss) border patt.
Rep the patt 7 more times.
Bind (cast) off in patt.

SIDE BORDERS
Using US 6 (4mm) needle and A and with RS facing, pick up and knit 177 stitches evenly along the side of the blanket, picking up across the ends of the borders as well as the patterned section. The best way to do this is to divide the edge into four equal sections marked with pins, then pick up 44 sts from each of three sections and 45 sts from one section.
Row 1: [K1, p1] to last st, k1.
Row 1 sets the seed (moss) border patt.
Rep the patt 7 more times
Bind (cast) off in patt.
Rep on other side edge.

TO MAKE UP
Weave in ends (see page 124).
Block knitting, pinning the edges out straight and following advice on ball band (see page 112).

ZIG-ZAG PATT
Join in C.
Row 1 (RS): Using C, k4, [sl1, k3] to marker, sm, sl1, sm, [k3, sl1] to last 4 sts, k4.
Row 2: Using C, p4, [sl1, p3] to marker, sm, sl1, sm, [p3, sl1] to last 4 sts, p4.
Row 3: Using B, k1, [sl1, k3] to 3 sts before marker, sl1, k5 (slipping markers), [sl1, k3] to last 2 sts, sl1, k1.
Row 4: Using B, p1, [sl1, p3] to 3 sts before marker, sl1, p5, (slipping markers), [sl1, p3] to last 2 sts, sl1, p1.
Row 5: Using C, k2, [sl1, k3] to last 3 sts, (slipping markers), sl1, k2.
Row 6: Using C, p2, [sl1, p3] to last 3 sts, (slipping markers), s|1, p2.
Row 7: Using B, [k3, sl1] to marker, sm, k1, sm, [sl1, k3] to end.
Row 8: Using B, [p3, sl1] to marker, sm, p1, sm, [sl1, p3] to end.

HOT WATER *Bottle Cozy*

This beautiful hot water bottle cozy is quicker to knit than you might think, and it has my favorite cable design running up the front of it. This cable looks a bit complicated, but it is actually just two mirror-image basic cables, so you could easily knit this even if you've not done much cabling before.

If you want to use a different bulky (chunky) yarn but can't find one that you love, try two strands of worsted (Aran) yarn held together. This will work just as well and gives you the option to splash out on something really luxurious and soft if you so desire.

To keep the design simple, there are no buttons or fastenings; the cover has a pillow-like design so you just slip the bottle in.

Yarn

Rowan Cocoon (80% merino wool, 20% kid mohair) bulky (chunky) yarn, 3½oz (100g), 76yd (70m) balls
2 balls in Alpine

Needles and equipment

1 pair of each of US 10 and 10½ (6.5 and 7mm) straight knitting needles
Cable needle
Large-eyed knitter's sewing needle

Size

11in (28cm) long and 8¼in (21cm) wide; rib neck 4in (10cm) long unrolled

Gauge (tension)

Project gauge (tension) of cable patt panel measures 4¼in (11cm) wide using US 10½ (7mm) needles.
Standard ball band gauge (tension) is 14 sts and 16 rows to 4in (10cm) over st st using US 10½ (7mm) needles.

Abbreviations

See page 126.
C10B = cable 10 back: C10F = cable 10 front: see page 120 for step-by-step illustrations.

WORKING CABLES

Every cable simply involves moving a group of stitches off the left-hand needle and working the next group on that needle first, followed by the ones you've moved. You either hold the stitches at the front or the back of your knitting while you knit the next group, so cables are either called F (front) or B (back) accordingly; (see page 120 for step-by-step instructions).

Any good knitting pattern will tell you how the cable should work, so you don't need to memorize every combination or permutation to cable routinely!

One thing to know is that in a written cable instruction—in this instance C10B and C10F—the 10 refers to the total number of stitches involved in the cable. You are generally only moving half of these stitches onto the cable needle.

Also, don't be too concerned about having a "official" cable needle; I don't have any. Pencils come in handy (as long as they are thinner than the needle you are using), but I mostly use any double-pointed needle that happens to be lying around: much more useful in the long run.

BACK

Using US 10 (6.5mm) needles, cast on 38 sts.
Row 1: [K2, p2] to last 2 sts, k2.
Row 2: [P2, k2] to last 2 sts, p2.
Rep rows 1–2 once more.
Change to US 10½ (7mm) needles.

START CABLE PATT
Row 1: K7, p2, k20, p2, k7.
Row 2 and all even-numbered rows: P7, k2, p20, k2, p7.
Row 3: K7, p2, C10B, C10F, p2, k7.
Row 4: As row 2.
Rep rows 1–2, 4 more times.
These 12 rows set the cable patt.
Rep the patt twice more.**

SHAPE TOP
Next row: As patt row 1.
Next row: P2tog, p5, k2, p20, k2, p5, p2tog. 36 sts
Next row: K2tog, k4, p2, C10B, C10F, p2, k4, k2tog. 34 sts
Next row: P5, k2, p20, k2, p5.
Next row: Bind (cast) off 7 sts, then k19, p2, k5. 27 sts
Next row: Bind (cast) off 7 sts, then k1, [p2, k2] to last 2 sts, p2. 20 sts

NECK RIB
Next row: [K2, p2] to end.
Rep last row 19 more times.
Bind (cast) off in patt.

FRONT
Complete as for Back to **.
Rep patt twice more, then rep rows 1–5
once more.

SHAPE TOP
Row 1: P2tog, p5, k2, p20, k2, p5,
p2tog. *36 sts*
Row 2: K2tog, k4, p2, k20, p2, k4,
k2tog. *34 sts*
Row 5: P5, k2, p20, k2, p5.
Row 6: Bind (cast) off 7 sts, then k19,
p2, k5. *27 sts*
Row 7: Bind (cast) off 7 sts, then k1, [p2,
k2] to last 2 sts, p2. *20 sts*

NECK RIB
Next row: [K2, p2] to end.
Rep last row 19 more times.
Bind (cast) off in patt.

TO MAKE UP
Weave in ends (see page 124).
Lay both pieces together with wrong sides
facing and matching the neck rib sections.
Sew up the side seams of the neck rib
section of the cover using backstitch (see
page 124): this means that the seam can't
be seen once the neck is rolled down.
Turn the cozy right side in. Pin the side
edges together down to the bottom edge
of the back piece. Measure 11in (28cm)
down the front piece, then fold the knitting
below that point over onto itself, right
sides together. Sew down each side edge
using backstitch, and sewing through all
three layers where the front piece is
folded over. Turn the cozy right side out.

HONEYCOMB *Pillow*

Honeycomb is another one of those stitch patterns that looks incredibly impressive, but is delightfully simple to create. And if you are new to color knitting, this slipstitch technique is a great place to start, because you are only ever dealing with one color of yarn at a time. Here, the pattern makes for a fabulous pillow cover with a simple garter stitch border. I have backed this pillow with fabric, but you could knit a back for yours if you prefer.

Yarn
Spud & Chloe Sweater (55% superwash wool, 45% organic cotton) worsted-weight (Aran) yarn, 3½oz (100g), 160yd (146m) skeins
  1 skein in Manatee (A)
  1 skein in Grape Jelly (B)

Other materials
16 x 16in (40 x 40cm) pillow pad
17 x 17in (43 x 43cm) of fabric
Sewing needle and thread to match fabric

Needles and equipment
1 pair of US 7 (4.5mm) straight knitting needles
Large-eyed knitter's sewing needle

Size
16 x 16in (40 x 40cm) over pillow pad, with ½in (1cm) border all around.

Gauge (tension)
Project gauge (tension) is 18 sts and 31 rows to 4in (10cm) over patt (unstretched) using US 7 (4.5mm) needles.
Standard ball band gauge (tension) is 16–20 sts to 4in (10cm) over st st using US 7–9 (4.5–5.5mm) needles.

Abbreviations
See page 126.
Note that all stitches are slipped purlwise (see page 113).

PILLOW FRONT
Using A, cast on 72 sts.
Knit 4 rows.
Join in B.
*Row 5 (RS): Using B, k3, [sl2, k6] to last 5 sts, sl2, k3.
Row 6: Using B, p3, [sl2, p6] to last 5 sts, sl2, p3.
Rep rows 5–6 twice more
Rows 11–14: Knit in A.
Row 15: Using B, k7, [sl2, k6] to last 9 sts, sl2, k7.
Row 16: Using B, p7, [sl2, p6] to last 9 sts, sl2, p7.
Rep rows 15–16 twice more.
Rows 21–24: Knit in A.*

BORDER
Using A, and starting at the bottom right-hand corner and with RS facing, pick up and knit about 70 sts to the top right-hand corner (see page 118). As a general rule, you should pick up three stitches for every four rows, but just make sure the pick-up looks neat, particularly over the garter stitch sections: you'll quickly get into a rhythm.
Knit 3 rows.
Bind (cast) off.
Rep along the opposite edge of the honeycomb panel.

TO MAKE UP
Weave in ends (see page 124).
Turn under a ½in (1cm) hem on all edges of the fabric. Wrong sides together, pin the fabric centrally to the honeycomb panel, leaving a border of garter stitch all the way around. Slipstitch the fabric to the knitting around three sides, the pop the pillow pad in and slipstitch the last edge closed.

KNITTING A PILLOW BACK

You can knit a plain stockinette (stocking) stitch back for your pillow. Using one color of Spud & Chloe Sweater yarn and US 7 (4.5mm) needles, cast on 72 sts. Work 116 rows in stockinette (stocking) stitch, then bind (cast) off. Slipstitch the edges of the back panel to the front panel, within the garter stitch border.

CHAPTER 2

To Wear

All the knits in this chapter are not only easy to make, they are also easy to wear. We love a relaxed, chic style with lots of color but with simple shapes and detailing, and that is what we have aimed for here. If you have never knitted a garment before, then you could start with the Short-Sleeved Sweater (see page 32), as it is not only very simple to knit, but because it doesn't have separate sleeves, it is also quick to make.

SUPER *Sloppy Joe*

This lovely, very sloppy sweater is knitted entirely in the round, from the top down. If you have never knitted in the round before, don't let that put you off. Using a chunky yarn is a great way of getting to grips with double-pointed needles and circular needles, and circular knitting is really a great way to deal with such bulk. And there are no seams to sew up!

Yarn

Mrs Moon Plump (80% superfine merino wool, 20% baby alpaca) super-bulky (super-chunky) yarn, 3½oz (100g), 76yd (70m) skeins

  4(5:6) skeins in Clotted Cream (A)

  1 skein in Rhubarb Crumble (B)

  1 skein in Marmalade (C)

Needles and equipment

Set of 4 double-pointed needles in each of US 17 (12mm) and US 19 (15mm)

US 17 (12mm) and US 19 (15mm) 24in (60cm) circular needles

US 19 (15mm) 32in (80cm) circular needle

4 round markers

Lengths of waste yarn for holding stitches

Large-eyed knitter's sewing needle

Size

To fit: small(medium:large)

To fit chest size: 35(39:43)in (90(99:110)cm)

Note that the sweater is designed to be a very baggy, loose fit.

FINISHED MEASUREMENTS

Chest: 42¼(44½:52½)in (107(113:133)cm)

Back neck to hem: 23(24:25)in (58.5(61:63.5)cm)

Gauge (tension)

Project gauge (tension) is 7 sts and 10 rows to 4in (10cm) over st st using US 19 (15mm) needles.

Standard ball band gauge (tension) is 10 sts and 10 rows to 4in (10cm) over st st using US 15 (10mm) needles.

Abbreviations

See page 126.

BODY

Using US 19 (15mm) 24in (60cm) circular needle and A, cast on 34(34:38) sts and join in the round, placing a marker to mark the beginning of the round.

Round 1: K4(4:5), pm, k13(13:14), pm, k4(4:5), pm, k13(13:14).

You have now marked the points for all the increases on the raglan sleeves. For orientation, the two longer sections are the front and back, the shorter sections are the sleeves.

Round 2: Knit.

Round 3: K1, m1r, *knit to the st before the next marker, m1l, k1, sm, k1, m1r, rep from * twice more, then knit to st before next marker, m1l, k1. 42 (42:46) sts

Rep rounds 2–3 until there are 114(122:142) sts in total; 24(26:31) across each sleeve, 33(35:40) across the back and front. Switch to the longer circular needle if necessary.

Next round: Knit.

DIVIDE FOR SLEEVES

Remove original markers as this round is worked.

Put the next 24(26:31) sts onto a length of waste yarn.

Using the backward loop cast on method (see page 108), cast on 2(2:3) sts, pm (to mark center of underarm) cast on 2(2:3) sts, knit to the next marker.

Put the next 24(26:31) sts onto a length of waste yarn.

Using the backward loop cast on method, cast on 2(2:3) sts, pm (to mark center of underarm) cast on 2(2:3) sts, knit across the 33(35:40) sts of the front. 74(78:92) sts

Cont to knit every round until the Body measures 19½(20½:21½)in (49.5(52:54.5)cm) from the cast-on edge, or the desired length.

ROUND MARKERS AND STITCH HOLDERS

You can use scraps of contrast color yarn as markers, but be careful not to lose concentration and knit them as though they were a stitch. It's a good idea to have two different colors; use one for the beginning of the round and a different color for the other markers.

When you use waste yarn to hold stitches, knot the ends of each length securely together to make sure the stitches don't fall off. It's a good idea to use a longer length of yarn than the stitches require, so you can try the sweater on when you are working out how long you want it to be.

*Change to B.
Next round: Knit.
Next round: Purl.
Rep last round 3 more times.
Change to C.
Next round: Knit.
Next round: Purl.
Rep last round twice more.
Next round: Knit.
Next round: Purl.
Bind (cast) off.
*If you would prefer a rib hem, cont to knit in A for 5 more rounds, then change to US 17 (12mm) circular needle and work 4 rounds of k1, p1 rib.

SLEEVE

(Both alike)
Divide the sleeve stitches evenly across 3 US 19 (15mm) double-pointed needles. Using the fourth needle and A, and starting at the center of the under arm, pick up and knit 2(2:3) sts, knit across the other sts and then at the end of the round, pick up a further 2(2:3) sts to complete the round at the center under arm, then place a marker. *28(30:37) sts*
Knit three rounds.
Next round: K1, k2tog, knit to last 3 sts, ssk, k1. *26(28:35) sts*
Knit 5 rounds.
Next round: K1, k2tog, knit to last 3 sts, ssk, k1. *24(26:33) sts*
Rep last six rounds 3 more times. *18(20:27) sts*
*Change to B.
Next round: Knit.
Next round: Purl.
Rep last round 3 more times.
Change to C.
Next round: Knit.
Next round: Purl.

Rep last round twice more.
Next round: Knit.
Next round: Purl.
Bind (cast) off.
*If you would prefer a rib cuff, cont to knit in A for 5 more rounds, then change to US 17 (12mm) double-pointed needles and work 4 rounds of k1, p1 rib.

NECK

The only slight downside of knitting a top-down sweater is that the neck is a bit tricky to make higher on the back than the front. We are now going to add this extra bit on so that you don't feel you've got the sweater on back to front all the time. With RS facing, US 17 (12mm) circular needle and A, and starting one stitch in from the back right shoulder increase, pick up and knit 11(11:12) sts across the back.
Turn, p11(11:12).
Next row: K11(11:12), then cont to knit around the neck of the sweater, picking up sts as folls (see also Picking Up Stitches, below): 3 sts across the back left raglan increases, 2(2:3) sts across the left shoulder, 3 sts across the front left raglan increases, 11(11:12) across the sweater front, 3 sts across front right raglan increases, 2(2:3) across right shoulder, then 3 sts across the back right raglan increases to complete the round. 38(38:42) sts.
Next round: [K1, p1] to end. (If you have picked up an odd number of sts, purl the last two sts of the round together.)
Rep the last round three times more.
Bind (cast) off in patt.
If you would rather have a polo or cowl neck, cont in rib until the neck is the required length. Then bind (cast) off.

TO MAKE UP

Weave in ends (see page 124).
Give the main sections of the sweater a gentle press.

PICKING UP STITCHES

It really depends on how your stitches look as to how many you should pick up across the increases: you want it to look neat, so don't stress if you feel you need to pick up more or fewer stitches. It doesn't matter how many you have in the end as long as the stitches are even and don't pull in or bulge out (see page 118).

SHORT-SLEEVED *Sweater*

This is a great first sweater project; I would thoroughly recommend giving it a go if you have not tried knitting a full garment before. It is knitted in the round from the top down, there are no stitches to pick up, only easy increases to work, and no boring sleeves to finish; so it takes no time to knit, and also is rather lovely!

Yarn

Mrs Moon Plump (80% superfine merino wool, 20% baby alpaca) super-bulky (super-chunky) yarn, 3½oz (100g), 76yd (70m) skeins
4(5:6) skeins in Lemon Curd

Needles and equipment

US 17 (12mm) 32in (80cm) circular needle
4 stitch markers (or scraps of yarn)
2 stitch holders (or lengths of yarn)
Large-eyed knitter's sewing needle

Size

To fit: S(M:L)

FINISHED MEASUREMENTS

Bust: 32(33¾:35½)in (81(86:90)cm)
Length: 17½(19:20)in (44(48:50.5)cm)

Gauge (tension)

Project gauge (tension) is 9 sts and 12 rows to 4in (10cm) over st st using US 17 (12mm) needles.
Standard ball band gauge (tension) is 10 sts and 10 rows to 4in (10cm) over st st using US 15 (10mm) needles.

Abbreviations

See page 126.

BODY

Cast on 56(56:56) sts and join in the round placing a marker at the beginning of the round.
Round 1: P10, pm, p18, pm, p10, pm, p18.
(10 sts for right sleeve, 18 sts for front, 10 sts for left sleeve, 18 sts for back.)
Round 2: [P1, inc, p to 2 sts before marker, inc, p1, sm] twice more, p1, inc, p to 2 sts before final marker, inc, p1, sm. *64 sts*
Round 3: Purl, slipping markers.
Rep rounds 2–3 7(8:9) times. *120(128:136) sts*
At this stage you can slip the knitting over your shoulders and check that it fits at the underarm. If you want your sweater a bit bigger, just keep increasing in the same way, but bear in mind that each pair of rounds adds about ⅝in (1.5cm), so don't work many rows before trying it on again. Purl one more round.

ROUND MARKERS AND STITCH HOLDERS

You can use scraps of contrast color yarn as markers, but be careful not to lose concentration and knit them as though they were a stitch. It's a good idea to have two different colors; use one for the beginning of the round and a different color for the other markers.

When you use waste yarn to hold stitches, knot the ends of each length securely together to make sure the stitches don't fall off. It's a good idea to use a longer length of yarn than the stitches require, so you can try the sweater on as you go.

SPLIT SLEEVES
Put the sts for right sleeve onto a stitch holder. Remove marker and cast on 1 st, place marker, cast on another st (this marker now marks the beginning and end of the round), knit to next marker, put the sts for left sleeve onto a holder, cast on 2 sts, knit to end of round.
Cont knitting until work measures 16¼(17¾:18¾)in (41(45:47.5)cm), or about 1¼in (3cm) shorter than your desired final length.
Next round: Purl.
Next round: Knit.
Next round: Purl.
Bind (cast) off.
With WS facing, put one set of arm stitches back on the needle.
Bind (cast) off.
Rep with other set of arm stitches.

TO MAKE UP
Weave in ends (see page 124).
Give the sweater a gentle press.

TANK *Top*

When we had our yarn store, at least once a week a customer would come in looking for a pattern for "a basic tank top" (vest top). I'm not sure whether it was just our leafy corner of London, or whether across the world this is something that people struggle to find, but it was always quite a desperate plea. I guess that tank tops are particularly suited to England's rather unpredictable weather: you're not committing to a full sweater, but can be confident that you're not going to freeze…! This pattern is hopefully that basic tank top that so many people want, and you can easily adapt the length by adding rows before the armhole decrease.

Yarn
Mrs Moon Plump DK (80% superfine merino wool, 20% baby alpaca) light-worsted-weight (double knitting) yarn, 1¾oz (50g), 125yd (115m) skeins
   5(6:6) skeins in Cherry Pie

Needles and equipment
1 pair of US 5 (3.75mm) straight knitting needles
1 pair of US 7 (4.5mm) straight knitting needles
US 5 (3.75mm) 24in (60cm) circular needle
Stitch holder
Large-eyed knitter's sewing needle

Size
To fit small (medium:large)

FINISHED MEASUREMENTS
Chest: 31(39½:47)in
(78.5(100.5:119)cm)
Back neck to hem: 21¾(23:24¼)in (55(58:61.5)cm)

Gauge (tension)
Project gauge (tension) is 21 sts and 27 rows to 4in (10cm) over st st using US 7 (4.5mm) needles.
Standard ball band gauge (tension) is 20–22 sts and 30 rows to 4in (10cm) over st st using US 6–7 (4–4.5mm) needles.

Abbreviations
See page 126.

BACK
*Using US 5 (3.75mm) straight needles, cast on 82(104:124) sts.
Row 1 (RS): [K1, p1] to end.
Row 1 sets the rib patt.
Rep row 1, 19 more times, or until rib measures 3in (7.5cm).
Change to US 7 (4.5mm) needles.
Row 21 (RS): Knit.
Row 22: Purl.
Rows 21–22 set st st.*
Cont in st st for 72(80:88) more rows, or until work measures 14(15:16)in (35.5(38:40.5)cm), finishing with a WS row.

SHAPE ARMHOLE
Next row: Bind (cast) off 2 sts, k to end. 80(102:122) sts

Next row: Bind (cast) off 2 sts, p to end. *78(100:120) sts*
Next row: K2, k2togtbl, k to last 4 sts, k2tog, k2.
76(98:118) sts
Next row: Purl.
Rep these last two rows 8(9:10) more times. *60(80:98) sts*
Starting with a k row, work 32 rows st st.

SHAPE BACK NECK AND SHOULDER

Next row (RS): K13(15:17) sts, bind (cast) off 34(50:64)
sts, k to end.
Cont to work on these last 13(15:17) sts only (left shoulder)
and place other 13(15:17) sts on a stitch holder.
Next row (WS): Bind (cast) off 4(6:8) sts, p to end. *9(9:9) sts*
Next row: Knit.
Next row: Bind (cast) off.
Put sts on holder onto needle and with WS facing, rejoin yarn,
p to end.
Next row (RS): Bind (cast) off 4(6:8) sts, k to end. *9(9:9) sts*
Next row: Purl.
Bind (cast) off.

FRONT

Work as for Back from * to *.
Cont in st st for 66(74:82) more rows, or until work measures
13(14:15)in (32.5(35:37.5cm), finishing with a WS row.
Next row (RS): K37(47:55), bind (cast) off 8(10:14) sts,
k to end.
Cont to work on these last sts only (right front) and place other
37(47:55) sts on a stitch holder.

SHAPE NECK AND ARMHOLE

Next row: P to last 2 sts, p2tog. *36(46:54) sts*
Next row: K2tog, k to end. *35(45:53) sts*
Rep last 2 rows twice more. *31(41:49) sts*
Next row: Bind (cast) off 2 sts, p to end. *29(39:47) sts*
Next row: K2tog, k to last 4 sts, k2tog, k2. *27(37:45) sts*
Next row: Purl.
Rep last 2 rows 6(9:10) more times. *15(21:25) sts*
First size only
Next row (RS): K to last 4 sts, k2tog, k2. *14 sts*
Next row: Purl.
Rep last 2 rows once more. *13 sts*
Second and Third sizes
Next row (RS): K2tog, k to end. *(18:24) sts*
Next row: Purl.
Rep last 2 rows (3:7) more times. *(15:17) sts*
All sizes
Cont in st st for 33(25:17) more rows.
Next row (WS): Bind (cast) off 4(6:8) sts, p to end. *9(9:9) sts*
Next row: Knit.
Next row: Bind (cast) off.
Put sts on holder onto needle and with WS facing, rejoin yarn.
Next row: P2tog, p to end. *36(46:54) sts*
Next row (RS): K to last 2 sts, k2tog. *35(45:53) sts*

Next row: P2tog, p to end. *34(44:52) sts*
Rep last 2 rows once more. *32(42:50) sts*
Next row: Bind (cast) off 2 sts, k to last 2 sts, k2tog. *29(39:47) sts*
Next row: Purl.
Next row: K2, k2togtbl, k to last 2 sts, k2tog. *27(37:45) sts*
Next row: Purl.
Rep last 2 rows 6(9:10) more times. *15(19:25) sts*
First size only
Next row (RS): K2, k2togtbl, k to end. *14 sts*
Next row: Purl.
Rep last 2 rows once more. *13 sts*
Second and Third sizes only
Next row (RS): K to last 2 sts, k2tog. *(18:24) sts*
Next row: Purl.
Rep these last two rows (3:7) more times. *(15:17) sts*
All sizes
Cont in st st for 34(26:18) more rows.
Next row: Bind (cast) off 4(6:8) sts, k to end. *9(9:9) sts*
Next row: Purl.
Bind (cast) off.

TO MAKE UP

Weave in ends (see page 124).
Block Back and Front following advice on ball band (see page
112), but avoid pressing the rib sections. Sew together the
corresponding shoulder seams and side seams using backstitch
(see page 124) or mattress stitch (see page 125), as preferred.

ARMHOLE RIB

With RS facing, using US 5 (3.75mm) circular needle, and
beginning at center underarm, pick up and knit 42(45:48) sts to
shoulder seam and 42(45:48) sts back down to center underarm.
Join in the round, placing a marker at the beginning of the round.
84(90:96) sts
Round 1: [K1, p1] to end.
Round 1 sets the rib patt.
Rep round 1, 3 more times.
Bind (cast) off.
Rep on other armhole.

NECK RIB

With RS facing, using US 5 (3.75mm) circular needle, and
beginning at left shoulder, pick up and knit 50(53:56) sts to the
bound (cast) off stitches at front, 8(10:14) sts across the bound
(cast) off stitches, 50(53:56) sts up to the right shoulder, 3 sts to
the bound (cast) off stitches at back, 34(50:64) across the bound
(cast) off stitches, and 3 sts up to the left shoulder. Join in the
round, placing a marker at the beginning of the round.
148(172:196) sts
Round 1: [K1, p1] to end.
Round 1 sets the rib patt.
Rep round 1, 3 more times.
Bind (cast) off.

I-CORD *Necklace*

I-cords are rather like French knitting, or finger knitting for grown-ups: little tubes of knitting that can be extremely handy for all sorts of things! They are far less fiddly to make than French knitting though, which is a real bonus. There are written instructions below, and step-by-step illustrated instructions on page 119.

This lovely necklace is simple and quick to knit, and can obviously be altered as much as you like. You can really have fun and use all sorts of yarns to create something really personal and unique. This is a great way to use up leftover yarn from almost any project, especially if the yarn is something special. The Platino yarn I have used is a beautifully soft metallic yarn that isn't at all scratchy.

Yarn

Mrs Moon Plump DK (80% superfine merino wool, 20% baby alpaca) light-worsted-weight (double knitting) yarn, 1¾oz (50g), 125yd (115m) skeins
   1 skein in Clotted Cream (A)
Lana Stop Platino (100% nylon) sport-weight (light double knitting) yarn, 1¾oz (50g), 208yd (200m) balls
   1 ball in Gold (B)

Other materials

Necklace clasp finding

Needles and equipment

2 US 6 (4mm) double-pointed needles
2 US 3 (3.25mm) double-pointed needles

Size

The i-cords of this necklace are all 20in (50cm) long, but you can make yours whatever length you wish.

Gauge (tension)

A precise gauge (tension) is not required for this project.
Standard ball band gauge (tension) for Mrs Moon Plump DK is 20–22 sts and 30 rows to 4in (10cm) over st st using US 6–7 (4–4.5mm) needles. Standard ball band gauge (tension) for Lana Stop Platino is 16 sts and 30 rows to 4in (10cm) over st st using US 6–7 (4–4.5mm) needles.

Abbreviations

See page 126.

HOW TO KNIT AN I-CORD

Cast on the required number of stitches onto one double-pointed needle. Knit one row. *Now, DO NOT TURN your knitting, but instead slide the stitches to the other end of the double-pointed needle that they are on. Pull the working yarn across behind the stitches and knit another row, knitting the first stitch firmly. Repeat from * and after a few rows you will begin to see the i-cord grow down from the needles. See also the step-by-step illustrated instructions on page 119.

I-CORD

Make five i-cords, following individual instructions.

FIRST I-CORD

Using A and US 6 (4mm) double-pointed needles, cast on 6 sts, leaving an 8in (20cm) tail of yarn before making the slip knot.
Knit i-cord until it measures 20in (50cm).
Bind (cast) off, leaving an 8in (20cm) end.

SECOND I-CORD

Using A and US 6 (4mm) double-pointed needles, cast on 3 sts, leaving an 8in (20cm) tail of yarn before making the slip knot.
Knit i-cord until it measures 20in (50cm).
Bind (cast) off, leaving an 8in (20cm) end.

THIRD I-CORD

Using B and US 3 (3.25mm) double-pointed needles, cast on 7 sts, leaving an 8in (20cm) tail of yarn before making the slip knot.
Knit i-cord until it measures 20in (50cm).
Bind (cast) off, leaving an 8in (20cm) end.

FOURTH I-CORD

Using B and US 3 (3.25mm) double-pointed needles, cast on 5 sts, leaving an 8in (20cm) tail of yarn before making the slip knot.
Knit i-cord until it measures 20in (50cm).
Bind (cast) off, leaving an 8in (20cm) end.

FIFTH I-CORD

Using B and US 3 (3.25mm) double-pointed needles, cast on 3 sts, leaving an 8in (20cm) tail of yarn before making the slip knot.
Knit i-cord until it measures 20in (50cm).
Bind (cast) off, leaving an 8in (20cm) end.

TO MAKE UP

Weave in ends (see page 124).
Work out how long you want your necklace to be, and trim the tails of yarn accordingly. Lay one end of each i-cord together and braid the tails (just split them into three groups of strands, it doesn't matter how many are in each group). Fix these ends into one half of the necklace clasp finding. Twist the i-cords together as you'd like them to lie, then braid the tails of yarn at the other ends and fix them into the other half of the clasp finding.

FLOATY *Tunic*

This fabulous, strappy tunic starts out billowing at the hem and gradually comes in to a flattering, slightly Jane Austen-esque empire line. I think those Georgians knew a bit about style; you can't go wrong with an empire line! And the best part is that all of the shaping is done using changes of knitting needle size, so you can knit this tunic without thinking. The beautiful yarn is incredibly soft and not at all itchy, and looks great using all sorts of needle sizes.

The tunic doesn't use much yarn, but it does use a lot of needles. I'd recommend investing in a set of interchangeable circular needles that you will use again and again.

Yarn

Rowan Mohair Haze (30% wool, 70% mohair) fingering (4-ply) yarn, ⅞oz (25g), 112yd (102m) balls
   3 balls in Comfort (A)
Blue Sky Alpacas Alpaca Silk (50% alpaca, 50% silk) sport-weight (double knitting) yarn, 1¾oz (50g), 146yd (133m) skeins
   1 skein in Blue (B)

Other materials

One ¼in (0.5cm) diameter button
Sewing needle and thread to match yarn B

Needles and equipment

1 of each of US 17, 15, 11, 10, 8, and 6 (12, 10, 8, 6, 5 and 4mm) circular 32in (80cm) needles
Large-eyed knitter's sewing needle
Stitch holder (or scrap of yarn)
Stitch marker (or length of yarn)

Size

To fit: S(M:L)

FINISHED MEASUREMENTS
Bust: 32(35½:39)in (81(90:99)cm) unstretched
Length without straps: 18(19:20)in (46(48:51)cm)

Gauge (tension)

Project gauge (tension) for Mohair Haze is 18 sts and 28 rows to 4in (10cm) over st st using US 8 (5mm) needles.
Project gauge (tension) for Alpaca Silk is 24 sts and 26 rows to 4in (10cm) over st st using US 5 (3.75mm) needles.
Standard ball band gauge (tension) for Mohair Haze is 28 sts and 36 rows to 4in (10cm) over st st using US 2–3 (3mm) needles.
Standard ball band gauge (tension) for Alpaca Silk is 20–24 sts to 4in (10cm) over st st using US 3–5 (3.25–3.75mm) needles.

Abbreviations

See page 126.

BODY

Using US 17 (12mm) needles and A, cast on 144(160:176) sts VERY loosely.
Join in the round, placing a marker at the beginning of the round.
Knit 7 rounds.
Change to US 15 (10mm) needles.
Knit every round until work measures 12in (30cm) from cast-on edge.
Change to US 11 (8mm) needles.
Knit every round for a further 3(4:5)in (8(10:13)cm).
Change to US 10 (6mm) needles.
Knit 5 rounds.
Change to US 8 (5mm) needles.
Knit 3 rounds.

SPLIT FOR OPENING

At this point turn the work and work back and forth in rows in st st on the circular needle.
Next row (WS): Purl.
Cont in st st (knit RS rows, purl WS rows) for 6 more rows.
Change to B.
Next row (RS): Knit.
Next row: [K1, p1] until 72(80:88) sts worked, pm, p to last 3 sts, k3.
Next row: K to marker, [k1, p1] to end.
Rep last 2 rows once more.
Next row: Bind (cast) off 72(80:88) sts to marker, p to last 3 sts, k3.

SHAPE FRONT BAND

Next row (dec): K2, k2tog, k to last 4 sts, k2tog, k2.
70(78:86) sts
Next row: K3, p to last 3 sts, k3.
Rep these last two rows twice more. 66(74: 82) sts
Change to US 6 (4mm) needles.
Row 1: K2tog, p2tog, [k1, p1] to last 4 sts, k2tog, p2tog.
62(70:78) sts
Row 2: [K1, p1] to end.
Rep these last two rows twice more. 54(62:70) sts

STRAPS

Next row: [K1, p1] 5 times, bind (cast) off until 9 sts rem on left-hand needle, [p1, k1] to last st, p1.
Cont to work the last 10 sts in k1, p1 rib patt as set until strap measures 15in (38cm) (or desired length). It's a good idea to try the tunic on to work out how long you need the straps, so put the 10 sts for the second strap on a stitch holder or scrap of yarn while you are working the first strap.
Bind (cast) off.
Put the 10 sts for the second strap back on the needles and work the second strap to match the first one.

TO MAKE UP

Sew the straps in place to the top edge of the back band.
Sew a button on the band at the top of the underarm opening. Make a loop from a scrap of B and attach to the other side for a buttonloop.

CHAPTER 3

For Children

The small scale and sheer cuteness make knits for kids so appealing. The projects in this chapter range from the oh-so-easy Wectangular Wabbit (see page 49), to the Funky Fair Isle Baby Cardigan (see page 46), which uses stranded color

knitting and has a chart to follow, but which is so small and is such a simple shape that you can really concentrate on the colorwork. If you need to rustle up a gift for a surprisingly early arrival then the Odds and Ends Ducks (see page 62) is the one for you, but if you have more time, then try one of the two blankets.

FUNKY FAIR ISLE *Baby Cardigan*

This fabulous cardigan uses a very simple Fair Isle pattern and is knitted from the top down, so you get to have some fun with color right at the start. You'll find it grows really quickly, and it is just such a satisfying, beautiful knit.

Special thanks to beautiful baby Esme who, as I was knitting this cardigan, endured various fittings with all the grace you would expect from such a gorgeous girl.

Yarn

Rowan Wool Cotton (50% merino wool, 50% cotton) light-worsted-weight (double knitting) yarn, 1¾oz (50g), 124yd (113m) balls

2(2:3) balls in Misty (A)
1 ball in Antique (B)
1 ball in Brolly (C)

Other materials

3 x ¼in (0.5cm) diameter buttons
Sewing needle and thread

Needles and equipment

US 2 (3mm), US 4 (3.5mm), and US 6 (4mm) knitting needles: circular needles are best because of the number of stitches involved, but you can use straight needles
4 x stitch markers (or scraps of yarn)
2 x stitch holders (or lengths of yarn)
Large-eyed knitter's sewing needle

Size

To fit: 3–6(6–12:12–18) months

FINISHED MEASUREMENTS
Underarm to hem: 5¼(6:6¾)in (13(15:17)cm)
Chest circumference: 21(23:27½)in (53(58.5:69.5)cm)

Gauge (tension)

Project gauge (tension) is 24 sts and 32 rows to 4in (10cm) over color patt using US 6 (4mm) needles.
Standard ball band gauge (tension) is 22–24 sts and 30–32 rows to 4in (10cm) over st st using US 5–6 (3.75–4mm) needles.

Abbreviations

See page 126.

BACK

Using US 2 (3mm) needles and A, cast on 70(78:86) sts.
Row 1: [K1, p1] to end
Row 1 sets the rib patt.
Rep row 1, 3 more times.
Change to US 4 (3.5mm) needles.
Row 5 (RS): K3, [k2, m1] to last 3 sts, k3. *102(114:126) sts*
Row 6: Purl.
Now follow chart, starting at bottom right-hand corner and working the first edge stitch, then the 4-st patt rep to the last st, then the other edge stitch. Keeping patt as set, work rows 1–4, then inc as folls:
Chart row 5: K2, [k3, m1] to last 4 sts, k4. *134(150:166) sts*
Cont to follow chart, working the first edge st, then the 4-st patt rep to the last st, then the other edge stitch
Chart row 10: Change to US 6 (4mm) needles.

CHART

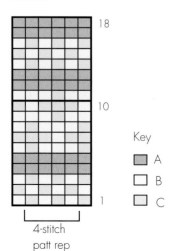

Key
- A
- B
- C

4-stitch patt rep

sts onto another stitch holder, cast on 2(4:6) sts, k to end. *126(139:165) sts*

Cont in st st (purl wrong-side rows, knit right-side rows), until work measures 4½(5¼:6)in (11(13:15)cm) from the underarm.

Change to US 4 (3.5mm) needles.

Next row: [K1, p1] to last 0(1:1) st, k0(1:1).

Next row: P0(1:1), [k1, p1] to end.

Rep last 2 rows once more.

Bind (cast) off.

SLEEVES

With RS facing, starting at the center of one set of underarm cast-on sts and using US 4 (3.5mm) needles and A, pick up and knit 1(2:3) sts, k across sts on holder, pick up and knit 2(2:3) more sts. *36(42:46) sts*

Row 1: [K1, p1] to end

Row 1 sets the rib patt.

Rep row 1 twice more.

Bind (cast) off.

Rep for other sleeve.

BUTTON BAND

LEFT FRONT

With RS facing, starting at the top and using US 4 (3.5mm) needles and A, pick up and knit 54(58:66) sts evenly along left-hand front.

Row 1: [K1, p1] to end

Row 1 sets the rib patt.

Rep row 1, 3 more times.

Bind (cast) off.

RIGHT FRONT

With RS facing, starting at the bottom and using US 4 (3.5mm) needles and A, pick up and knit 54(58:66) sts evenly along right-hand front.

Row 1: [K1, p1] to end.

Row 2 (buttonholes): [K1, p1] to last 20 sts, yo, k2tog, [k1, p1] 3 times, yo, k2tog, [k1, p1] 3 times, yo, k2tog, k1, p1.

Row 3: [K1, p1] to end.

Rep row 3 once more.

Bind (cast) off.

TO MAKE UP

Weave in ends (see page 124).

Block knitting following advice on ball band (see page 112).

Join edges of sleeve ribbing. Sew on buttons.

Chart row 18: P1(3:2) [m1, p6] to last 1(3:2) sts, 0(1:0), p1(3:2). *156(175:193) sts*

Break B and C and cont in A.

Next row: K25(26:32), m1, k1, pm, k1, m1, k23(28:28), m1, k1, pm, k1, m1, k52(59:65), m1, k1, pm, k1, m1, k23(28:28), m1, k1, pm, k1, m1, k to end. *164(183:201) sts*

Next row: Purl.

Next row: [K to 1 st before marker, m1, k1, sm, k1, m1] 4 times, k to end.

Rep these last two rows 2(2:3) more times. *188(207:233) sts*

Next row: Purl.

SPLIT FOR SLEEVES

Next row: Removing markers when reached, k to first marker, slip the next 33(38:40) sts onto a stitch holder, cast on 2(4:6) sts, k to marker at start of second sleeve, slip the next 33(38:40)

WECTANGULAR *Wabbit*

This lovely little rabbit is designed to be knitted by a beginner knitter—if you have learned the knit and purl stitches, then this one is for you. There is absolutely no shaping, fancy sewing up, or difficult features to manage, and it's a lovely knit for an adult or a child. Each section uses a different stitch pattern, so you can get to grips with mixing knits and purls, and you can play around with the design as much as you fancy.

I find I get ridiculously attached to knitted toys; as soon as they have features I feel very protective about them. It's a bit like giving birth, but much less painful and a lot less work once they're "born," so enjoy making your Wabbit exactly as you'd like him/her to be!

Yarn

Spud & Chloe Sweater (55% superwash wool, 45% organic cotton) worsted-weight (Aran) yarn, 3½oz (100g), 160yd (146m) skeins
  1 skein in Chocolate Milk
Small amounts of cream and pink worsted-weight (Aran) or light-worsted-weight (double knitting) yarn for the pocket, tail, and features

Other materials

Toy stuffing

Needles and equipment

US 7 (4.5mm) straight knitting needles
1 stitch holder
Large-eyed knitter's sewing needle
Mini pom-pom maker (optional)

Size

Top of ear to toe: 19in (48cm)
Shoulder to toe: 13in (33cm)
Width across tummy: 5in (13cm)

Gauge (tension)

Project gauge (tension) is 18 sts and 20 rows to 4in (10cm) over st st using US 7 (4.5mm) needles.
Standard ball band gauge (tension) is 4–5 sts to 4in (10cm) over st st using US 7–9 (4.5–5.5mm) needles.

Abbreviations

See page 126.

BACK

*Cast on 20 sts.
Starting at bottom of body, knit 46 rows.

SHAPE HEAD
Row 47 (RS): Bind (cast) off 3 sts, k to end. *17 sts*
Row 48: Bind (cast) off 3 sts, p to end. *14 sts*
Row 49: Knit.
Row 50: Purl.
Rep rows 49–50, 5 more times.*
Bind (cast) off.

FRONT
Work as for Back from * to *.

SPLIT FOR EARS
Next row (RS): Bind (cast) off 1 st, then [p1, k1] twice,
(5 sts on right-hand needle), bind (cast) off 2 sts, then
[p1, k1] twice, p1.
Next row: Bind (cast) off 1 st, then [p1, k1] twice, put
rem unworked 5 sts on stitch holder.

RIGHT EAR
Next row: [K1, p1] twice, k1.
Rep this last row 30 more times.
Bind (cast) off in patt.

LEFT EAR
Put the 5 sts on the stitch holder back on the needles
with the WS facing for the next row.
Next row: [K1, p1] twice, k1.
Rep this last row 31 more times.
Bind (cast) off in patt.

LEGS
Make 2
Cast on 8 sts.
Knit 96 rows.
Bind (cast) off.

ARMS
Make 2
Cast on 10 sts.

Row 1: [K1, p1] to end.
Rep row 1, 28 more times.
Bind (cast) off.

POCKET
Using pink yarn, cast on 12 sts.
Row 1: Purl.
Row 2: Knit.
Rep rows 1–2, 3 more times.
Next row: Purl.
Next row (rib): * K1, p1, rep from * to end.
Rep last row twice more.
Bind (cast) off.

TO MAKE UP
Begin with the legs. Fold each leg in half lengthwise and sew up
the long edge using a simple oversewing stitch (see page 124).
You will need to stuff the legs as you sew to make it easier to get
the stuffing to the bottom. Once stuffed as much as you want
(you want the top of the legs to be flat, so don't over-fill them),
sew across the top edges.
Sew and stuff both arms in the same way.
Make a pom-pom. Wind cream yarn around two fingers about
20 times. Slip the bundle off your fingers and tie a length of yarn
round the middle of it, tying and knotting it tightly. Using
scissors, cut the loops at either end of the bundle, fluff up the
pom-pom, and trim any long ends to make a pom-pom about ¾in
(2cm) across. Use the ends of the tying yarn to sew the pom-pom
to the center of the rabbit's back, about 1¼in (3cm) up from the
bottom edge. Alternatively, use a mini pom-pom maker.
Using oversewing stitch, sew the pocket to the front of the
rabbit's body.
Assembling the body is just a tiny bit fiddly, but the "naïve"
finished result allows for a relaxed approach in my opinion! I
find it best to start by sewing up the bottom edges and the legs
first. Lay the back flat and right-side down and space the legs as
you'd like them to hang down from the bottom edge. Lay the
front on top, right side up, sandwiching the tops of the legs
between the front and back, and pin the layers together.
Oversew the front and back together until you get to the first leg,
then backstitch (see page 124) across the leg sewing through
the two body pieces. Oversew between the legs, backstitch
across the other leg, and oversew the rest of the bottom edge.
Oversew the side seams, positioning the tops of the arms
about 1¼in (3cm) down from the shoulders and backstitching
across them in the same way as for the legs. Stuff the body as
you go. Oversew the shoulders, and then work a line of simple
running stitch across the bottom of the head, just to separate it
from the body.
Using contrast yarns (I used cream for the eyes and pink for the
mouth, but you could use any colors you like), embroider a
single cross stitch for each eye and for the mouth.
Oversew round the edges of the head, stuffing it as you go.
Give your rabbit a squeeze and a name.

CIRCULAR *Baby Blanket*

This baby blanket is fun to do, and it just grows and grows. You start with a small number of stitches at the center, increase at the same points on each round, and stop when you run out of yarn. If you haven't knitted in the round before, there are illustrated instructions on page 118. I've gone for traditional girlie colors, but you could go for blues, or for rainbow hues as the need requires!

Yarn
Spud & Chloe Sweater (55% superwash wool, 45% organic cotton) worsted-weight (Aran) yarn, 3½oz (100g), 160yd (146m) skeins
- 1 skein in Tiny Dancer (A)
- 1 skein in Igloo (B)
- 1 skein in Watermelon (C)
- 1 skein in Jelly Bean (D)
- 1 skein in Popsicle (E)
- 1 skein in Barn (F)
- 1 skein in Grape Jelly (G)

Needles and equipment
US 8 (5mm) 32in (80cm) circular needle
Set of 4 US 8 (5mm) double-pointed needles
5 round markers
Large-eyed knitter's sewing needle

Size
Center to straight edge: 14in (35.5cm)

Gauge (tension)
Project gauge (tension) is 18 sts and 23 rows to 4in (10cm) over st st using US 8 (5mm) needles.
Standard ball band gauge (tension) is 16–20 sts to 4in (10cm) over st st using US 7–9 (4.5–5.5mm) needles.

Abbreviations
See page 126.

BLANKET
Using US 8 (5mm) double-pointed needles and A, cast on 10 sts. Divide the stitches over 3 needles (3, 3, 4 sts on each needle) and join in the round, placing a marker at the beginning of the round.
Round 1 (RS): [Inc] in every st. *20 sts*
Round 2: [Inc, k3, pm] to last 4 sts, inc, k3. *25 sts*
Round 3: [Inc, k to marker, sm] to end. *30 sts*
Round 3 sets the patt.
Cont in patt, slipping sts and markers onto circular needle when there are too many sts to fit comfortably onto the dpns.
Work 6 more rounds in patt. *60 sts*
Change to B.
Work 3 rounds in patt. *75 sts*
Change to C.
Work 11 rounds in patt. *130 sts*
Change to B.
Work 3 rounds in patt. *145 sts*
Change to D.
Work 11 rounds in patt. *200 sts*
Change to B.
Work 3 rounds in patt. *215 sts*
Change to E.
Work 11 rounds in patt. *270 sts*
Change to B.
Work 3 rounds in patt. *285 sts*
Change to F.
Work 11 rounds in patt. *340 sts*
Change to B.
Work 3 rounds in patt. *355 sts*
Change to G.
Work 11 rounds in patt. *410 sts*
Change to B.
Work 3 rounds in patt. *425 sts*
Bind (cast) off.

TO MAKE UP
Weave in ends (see page 124).
Block blanket as directed on the ball band (see page 112).

ROUND MARKERS

You can use scraps of contrast color yarn as round markers, but be careful not to lose concentration and knit them as though they were stitches. It's a good idea to have two different colors; use one for the marker at the beginning of the round and a different color for the four other markers.

CHILD'S *Muff*

I love knitting loops! I am still fascinated by how they work and I just love the fun look they create. This muff has vintage boho echoes of the 1970s, and reminds me of being a child during that flamboyant decade. But it is also actually really practical; no more cold tiny hands or lost mittens!

Yarn
Rooster Aran (50% merino wool, 50% baby alpaca) worsted-weight (Aran) yarn, 1¾oz (50g), 103yd (94m) balls
2 balls in Lagoon (A) (this yarn is used double, one end from each ball)
1 ball in Shimmer (B)

Needles and equipment
1 pair of US 10½ (6.5mm) straight knitting needles
2 US 6 (4mm) double-pointed needles
Large-eyed knitter's sewing needle
Sewing needle and thread to match yarn

Size
6¾in high x 8¾in wide (17cm high x 22cm wide), excluding cord

Gauge (tension)
Project gauge (tension) is 13 sts and 16 rows to 4in (10cm) over st st using US 10½ (6.5mm) needles and two strands of yarn.
Standard ball band gauge (tension) is 19 sts and 23 rows to 4in (10cm) over st st using US 7–9 (4.5–5.5mm) needles and one strand of yarn.

Abbreviations
See page 126.
ML = make loop: see page 121 for step-by-step instructions.

MAIN PART
Using US 10½ (6.5mm) needles and one end from each ball of A held together as one, cast on 29 sts.
Row 1: [ML, k1] to last st, ML.
Row 2 (RS): Knit.
Row 3: [K1, ML] to last st, k1.
Row 4: As row 2.
Rep rows 1–4 until work measures 7in (18cm) from cast-on edge, finishing with a RS row, then, beg with a purl row, cont in st st for another 7in (18cm).
Bind (cast) off.

TO MAKE UP
Weave in ends (see page 124).
With RS facing in and using backstitch (see page 124), sew the cast-on and bound- (cast-) off edges together. The loopy side of the muff is the front and the plain st st side is the back.

CORD
Using one strand of B, knit an i-cord (see page 119) that is about 39in (100cm) long (or as long as required). Starting at the bottom of the muff, sew one end of the i-cord to the side of the st st back panel, fastening off firmly at the top of that panel. Sew the other end of the cord to the other side of the panel in the same way.

CHILD'S *Simple Sweater*

This wonderfully basic sweater is a great first garment project. As it is knitted entirely in garter stitch it is quite yarn hungry, but it's very quick to knit up and makes a fabulous snuggly layer for a child.

In my opinion, the only downside to knitting a sweater like this is that it can be tricky to sew up really chunky yarn tidily, so, I've used a three-needle bind (cast) off on the shoulders. This makes for a beautifully neat and secure shoulder seam, and I really recommend giving it a go—it's extremely easy and really rather satisfying!

Take care to make a note of how many rows you have knitted on the front and back pieces before the armhole shaping, so that when you come to sew the pieces together you can get the seam looking as neat as possible.

Yarn

Mrs Moon Plump (80% superfine merino wool, 20% baby alpaca) super-bulky (super-chunky) yarn, 3½oz (100g), 76yd (70m) skeins

  5(6:7) skeins in Fondant Fancy

Needles and equipment

1 pair of US 15 (10mm) straight knitting needles

US 15 (10mm) 16in (40cm) circular needle (or set of 4 US 15 (10mm) long double-pointed needles)

Four stitch holders (or waste yarn)

Large-eyed knitter's sewing needle

Two round markers

Size

To fit: 5–6(7–8:9–10) years

To fit chest size: 27½(28½:29)in (70(72:74)cm)

FINISHED MEASUREMENTS

Back neck to hem: 17¾(19:21)in (45(48:53)cm)

Gauge (tension)

Project gauge (tension) is 10 sts and 15½ rows to 4in (10cm) over garter stitch using US 15 (10mm) needles.

Standard ball band gauge (tension) is 10 sts and 10 rows to 4in (10cm) over st st using US 15 (10mm) needles.

Abbreviations

See page 126.

BACK

*Cast on 36(38:40) sts loosely.

Knit 41(44:47) rows, or until work measures 10½(11:12¼)in (27(28:31)cm).

SHAPE ARMHOLE

Next row: Bind (cast) off 2(2:2) sts, knit to end. *34(36:38) sts*

Next row: Bind (cast) off 2(2:2) sts, knit to end. *32(34:36) sts*

Knit 25(28:31) rows, or until armhole measures 6½(7¼:8)in (16(18:20)cm) from start of shaping.

SHAPE NECK

Next row: K6(7:8), bind (cast) off 20 sts, knit to end.

Next row: K6(7:8); put the second set of 6(7:8) sts on a stitch holder (or length of waste yarn).

Next row: K6(7:8); put these sts on a stitch holder (or length of waste yarn).

Now put the first set of 6(7:8) sts back on a needle and re-join yarn next to bound (cast) off sts.

Knit 2 rows; put these stitches back on a stitch holder (or length of waste yarn).

FRONT

Work as for Back from * to *.

Knit 20(23:26) rows, or until armhole measures 5¼(6:6¾)in (13(15:17)cm) from start of shaping.

SHAPE NECK
Next row: K7(8:9), bind (cast) off 18 sts, knit to end.
Next row: K5(6:7), k2tog; put the second set of 7(8:9) sts on a stitch holder (or length of waste yarn).
Knit 6 rows; put these sts on a stitch holder (or length of waste yarn).
Now put the first set of 7(8:9) sts back on a needle and re-join yarn next to bound (cast) off sts.
Next row: K2tog, knit to end.
Knit 6 rows; put these stitches back on a stitch holder (or length of waste yarn).
I find it's a good idea to join the front and back together now, before you forget which bit goes where. As both pieces are reversible, check which side of each piece is neatest and sew in the ends (see page 124) on the other side (now the reverse side).
RS together, lay the front on top of the back. Now slip the 7(8:9) sts from one shoulder of the Back onto a needle and then the 7(8:9) sts from the same shoulder of the Front onto another needle, making sure both needles point in the same direction. Rejoin the yarn to the Front piece, and hold these needles together in your left hand. Insert another needle into the first stitch of the front needle, then the first stitch of the back needle. Knit these 2 sts together. Do the same with the second stitch on each needle. Now lift the first stitch on the right-hand needle over the second stitch, as for a standard bind (cast) off. Cont to bind (cast) off these two sets of stitches together until you have just one stitch left. Break the yarn and fasten off.
Rep for the other shoulder.

SLEEVE
Make 2
Cast on 20 sts.
Knit 5 rows.

Next row: Inc, knit to last st, inc. *22 sts*
Rep the last six rows 7(9:11) more times. *36(40:44) sts*
Knit 10 rows.
Bind (cast) off.

TO MAKE UP
RS together, pin a bound- (cast-) off edge of the sleeve to an armhole of the body: the top of the arm should fit between the armhole shapings. Using backstitch (see page 124), sew the top of the sleeve in place. If you sew with the sleeve uppermost, you can make sure that you always sew into the same row to keep the sewing lovely and neat.
Rep for the other sleeve.
RS facing in, fold the sweater along the shoulders and match the side and underarm seams. Using backstitch sew up those seams, matching the row ends on each piece for the neatest finish.
Weave in ends (see page 124).

NECKBAND
Using a US 15 (10mm) 16in (40cm) circular needle (or long double-pointed needles), and starting at the left shoulder seam, pick up and knit 22 sts evenly across the Front, place marker, pick up and knit 18 sts evenly across the Back, place marker, and join in the round. *40 sts*
Round 1: [K1, p1] to end.
Round 2: [K1, p1] to last 2 sts, k2tog. *39 sts*
Round 3: P2tog, [k1, p1] to 2 sts before next marker, k2tog, p2tog, [k1, p1] to last 3 sts, k1, p2tog. *35 sts*
Bind (cast) off.
Weave in ends (see page 124).

CHECKED *Baby Blanket*

This blanket looks complicated, but in fact uses a really easy slipstitch pattern that means you are only ever working with one color at a time. The soft cotton yarn is used double, giving the blanket a lovely "squish" and extra warmth. The border is knitted on after the main section has been completed, and with no tricky mitered corners, so this really is a simple knit. The size of the finished blanket makes it perfect for using in a pram or stroller.

Yarn
Blue Sky Alpacas Worsted Cotton (100% organic cotton) worsted-weight (Aran) yarn, 3½oz (100g), 150yd (137m) skeins
  2 skeins in Shell (A)
  2 skeins in Lemonade (B)
  3 skeins in Lemongrass (C)

Needles and equipment
US 11 (8mm) 32in (80cm) circular needle
Large-eyed knitter's sewing needle

Size
29¼ x 27in (74 x 68cm)

Gauge (tension)
Project gauge (tension) is 11 sts and 14 rows to 4in (10cm) over st st using US 11 (8mm) needles and two strands of yarn.
Standard ball band gauge (tension) is 16–20 sts and 22–24 rows to 4in (10cm) over st st using US 7–9 (4.5–5.5mm) needles and one strand of yarn.

Abbreviations
See page 126.
Note that all stitches are slipped purlwise (see page 113).

WINDING THE YARN
The whole blanket is knitted using the yarn doubled. You will need to wind all the balls of yarn making sure you can pull the ends from the center and the outside at the same time. If you don't have a ball winder (I don't, so don't be put off), you just need to wind it in such a way that both ends are free.

MAIN PART
Using 2 strands of A held together as one, cast on 90 sts.
Row 1: Using A, purl.
Row 2 (RS): Using B, k1, sl1, [k2, sl2] to last 4 sts, k2, sl1, k1.
Row 3: Using B, p1, sl1, [p2, sl2] to last 4 sts, p2, sl1, p1.
Row 4: Using A, knit.
Row 5: Using C, [p2, sl2] to last 2 sts, p2.
Row 6: Using C, [k2, sl2] to last 2 sts, k2.
These 6 rows set the check patt and are repeated throughout.

HANDLING THE YARNS

You are only ever using one color yarn at a time. When slipping stitches, you always slip them as if you are going to purl them, that is, put your needle in from right to left, without twisting the stitches. Be careful not to pull the yarn too tight behind the slipped stitches. As all three yarns will be attached to your work throughout, be vigilant about not tangling them up—it will save you hours of unknotting!

Always leave the colors that you are not using attached and just start using them as required, making sure that you don't pull them too tight either up the side or behind the slipped stitches. Don't worry if the edges look a bit messy, the border will hide them!
Cont in check patt until the blanket has reached the desired length (mine measures 27in (68cm) long).
Bind (cast) off on a color A row.
Before adding the border, block the knitting to even all the stitches out (see page 112).

BORDER
Using C double, and starting in the top right-hand corner, pick up and knit 90 stitches evenly across the top of the blanket.
Knit 3 rows.
Bind (cast) off.
Rep on the bottom edge.
Starting at the bottom right-hand corner (the outer edge of the new border), pick up and knit 74 stitches evenly along to the outer edge of the opposite border. As a general rule, when picking up stitches along the side of your knitting you should pick up 3 stitches for every 4 rows (see page 118). Don't be too worried about the exact number; the most important thing is that the border lies flat. Make sure that you pick up the stitches in the same place along the row so that you get a lovely straight line.
Rep on the other side.

TO MAKE UP
Weave in ends (see page 124).
Block knitting following advice on ball band (see page 112).

ODDS AND ENDS *Ducks*

These super-simple, super-quick-to-knit ducks will be my go-to baby gift from now on! I always try to use the best yarn possible for a project, but lovely yarns do obviously come at a price and it is desperate to have lots of odds and ends left over. The baby cardigan on page 46 is a case in point, as there will be quite a lot of the contrast color yarns left: making some adorable ducks and ducklings is a great way of using up those yarns.

This pattern works for any weight of yarn, just use the needles recommended on the yarn's ball band and follow the pattern. The big duck shown here is made in Mrs Moon Plump. You can create a menagerie of different-sized birds that you could then string together to make a mobile.

Yarn
Mrs Moon Plump (80% superfine merino wool, 20% baby alpaca) super-bulky (super-chunky) yarn, 3½oz (100g), 76yd (70m) skeins
  About ¾oz (25g) in Lemon Curd (A)
  About ¼oz (8g) in Marmalade (B)
Scraps of dark-colored yarn for eyes

Other materials
Small amount of toy stuffing

Needles and equipment
1 pair of US 15 (10mm) straight knitting needles
Large-eyed knitter's sewing needle

Size
6¾in (17cm) long and 4½in (11.5cm) high

Gauge (tension)
Project gauge (tension) is 10 sts and 10 rows to 4in (10cm) over st st using US 15 (10mm) needles. Standard ball band gauge (tension) is 10 sts and 10 rows to 4in (10cm) over st st using US 17 (12mm) needles.

Abbreviations
See page 126.

RIGHT BODY
*Using A, cast on 10 sts.
Row 1: Purl.
Row 2: Inc, k to last st, inc. *12 sts*
Row 3: Purl.
Rep rows 2–3, 3 more times. *18 sts*
Row 10: K7, bind (cast) off 8 sts, k to end.
Turn and work first 3 sts only for tail.

WINGS

Make 2
Using B, cast on 7 sts.
Row 1: Knit.
Row 2: K2tog, k to end. *6 sts*
Row 3: K to last 2 sts, k2tog. *5 sts*
Rep rows 2–3 once more, then rep row 2 once more. *2 sts*
Next row: K2tog and fasten off.

TO MAKE UP

Weave in ends (see page 124).
With right sides facing and using backstitch (see page 124), sew the two body pieces together, leaving the bottom cast-on edge open. Turn the duck the right way out and stuff as desired. Using mattress stitch (see page 125), sew the bottom seam.
Position the wings as desired on body and sew in place. Using a scrap of dark-colored yarn, embroider straight stitches for the eyes. Using B, oversew across front of head several times to create a beak.

Row 11: Purl.
Row 12: K2tog, k1. *2 sts*
Row 13: P2tog and fasten off.

HEAD
With WS facing, rejoin yarn.
Next row: Purl.
Next row: Knit.
Next row: Purl.
Next row: K2tog, k3, k2tog. *5 sts*
Next row: Purl.
Bind (cast) off.

LEFT BODY

Work as for Right Body from * to *.
Row 10: K3, bind (cast) off 8 sts, k6.
Turn and work first 7 sts only for head.
Row 11: Purl.
Row 12: Knit.
Row 13: Purl.
Row 14: K2tog, k3, k2tog. *5 sts*
Row 15: Purl.
Bind (cast) off.

TAIL
With WS facing, re-join yarn.
Next row: Purl.
Next row: K1, k2tog. *2 sts*
Next row: P2tog and fasten off.

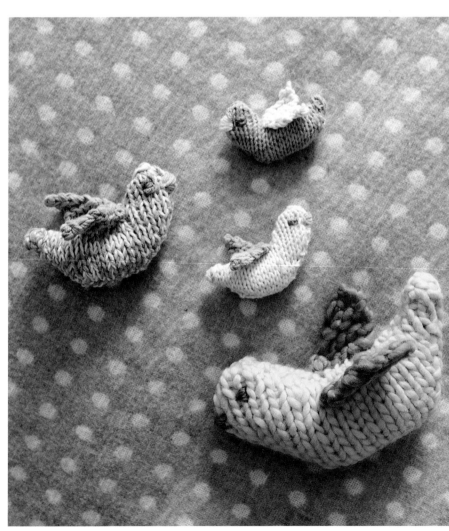

PIXIE *Baby Hat*

This cute hat is a perfect last-minute gift for a baby, so ideal if you won't know if the newbie will be a boy or a girl. Once you have mastered knitting in the round, the hat takes just an evening to complete, so as soon as you hear the news you can whip one up in a suitable color and present it to the little one the following day. (I speak from experience, having done this many times!) And if you haven't knitted in the round or worked an i-cord before, there are illustrated instructions on page 118 and page 119.

Any light worsted-weight (DK) yarn will do for this hat, but something washable is a good idea, and, of course, the yarn must be beautifully soft. Big Bad Wool Weepaca fits all the above criteria, and is just gorgeous!

Yarn

Big Bad Wool Weepaca (50% fine washable merino, 50% baby alpaca) light-worsted-weight (double knitting) yarn, 1¾oz (50g), 95yd (86m) skeins
    1 skein in Coral
Small amount of contrasting yarn for pom-pom

Needles and equipment

Set of 5 US 7 (4.5mm) double-pointed needles
1 round marker
Large-eyed knitter's sewing needle
Two circles of card, each measuring 1½in (4cm) in diameter with a central hole ¾in (2cm) in diameter, or a mini pom-pom maker

Size

To fit: 0–6(6–12) months

Finished measurements

Circumference: 11¼(12¾)in (29.5(32)cm)
Height including pom-pom and with brim rolled back: 9½(10)in (24.5(26)cm)

Gauge (tension)

Project gauge (tension) is 20 sts and 26 rows to 4in (10cm) over st st using US 7 (4.5mm) needles.
Standard ball band gauge (tension) is 18–22 sts and 25–28 rows to 4in (10cm) over st st using US 5–7 (3.75–4.5mm) needles.

Abbreviations

See page 126.

HAT

Cast on 56(64) sts.
Divide the stitches over 4 needles, 14(16) sts on each needle, and join in the round, placing a marker at the beg of the round.
Knit 30(33) rounds, or until work measures 4½(5)in (11.5(13)cm) from cast-on edge.

SHAPE CROWN

Next round: [K2tog, k6] to end. 49(56) sts
Next round: [K2tog, k5] to end. 42(48) sts

Next round: [K2tog, k4] to end.
35(40) sts
Next round: [K2tog, k3] to end.
28(32) sts
Knit 2 rounds.
Next round: [K2tog, k2] to end.
21(24) sts
Knit 4 rounds.
Next round: [K2tog, k1] to end.
14(16) sts
Knit 6 more rounds.
Next round: K2tog to end. *7(8) sts*
Knit 3 rounds.
0–6 months
Next round: [K2tog] to last st, k1. *4 sts*
6–12 months
Next round: [K2tog] to end. *4 sts*
Both sizes
Now work in i-cord for 10 rows (or as long as desired).
Bind (cast) off.

TO MAKE UP

Weave in ends (see page 124).
Press the knitting as directed on the ball band.

Make a pom-pom. Place the two card circles together and wind contrast color yarn around and through the central hole until the hole is filled. Using scissors, cut through the yarn wraps around the edges of the circles. Tie a length of yarn round the bundle of strands, between the circles, tying and knotting it tightly. Remove the card circles, fluff up the pom-pom, and trim any long ends. Alternatively, use a mini pom-pom maker. Use the ends of the tying yarn to sew the pom-pom to the end of the i-cord.

ROUND MARKERS

You can use a scrap of yarn as a marker, but be careful not to lose concentration and knit it as though it was a stitch.

NUMBER *Blanket*

This color knitting project combines both intarsia (see page 123) and stranding (see page 122). You strand the main yarn across the back of the number stitches, but then drop the number color as you move along the row to the next number. The trickiest part is making sure that all the yarns don't get tangled up—be vigilant about untangling the balls at the end of each row.

Once the blanket edge is set up, you follow the chart on page 69. As with all charts, you start at the bottom right-hand corner, and for this project you knit all right-side rows and purl all wrong-side rows. The blanket will look fantastic in any nursery and because the yarn is nice and chunky you can watch it grow quickly, which is very satisfying!

Yarn
Debbie Bliss Roma (70% wool, 30% alpaca) super-bulky (super-chunky) yarn, 3½oz (100g), 87yd (80m) balls
- 2 balls in Ecru (A)
- 1 ball in Teal (B)
- 1 ball in Apple (C)
- 1 ball in Citrus (D)
- 1 ball in Hot Pink (E)
- 1 ball in Crimson (F)

Needles and equipment
1 pair of US 17 (12mm) straight knitting needles
US 17 (12mm) 32in (80cm) circular needle
Large-eyed knitter's sewing needle

Size
27½ x 29½in (70 x 75cm)

Gauge (tension)
Project gauge (tension) is 9 sts and 12 rows to 4in (10cm) over st st using US 17 (12mm) needles.
Standard ball band gauge (tension) is 9 sts and 12 rows to 4in (10cm) over st st using US 17 (12mm) needles.

Abbreviations
See page 126.

BLANKET

BOTTOM BORDER
Using F and straight needles, cast on 51 sts.
Knit 2 rows.
Change to E.
Knit 2 rows.
Change to D.
Knit 2 rows.

SIDE BORDER

With RS facing and using US 17 (12mm) circular needle and B, evenly pick up and knit 70 sts. The best way to do this is to divide the edge into four equal sections marked with pins, then pick up 18 sts from each of two sections and 17 sts from each of two sections.

Knit one row.
Change to C.
Knit 2 rows.
Change to D.
Knit 2 rows.
Change to E.
Knit 2 rows.
Change to F.
Knit 2 rows.
Bind (cast) off.
Rep down other side.

TO MAKE UP

Weave in ends (see page 124).
Press as directed on the ball band.
If you wish, you can sew a fabric backing to the blanket, leaving the border free around the edges. This will be nice and neat and means you can be less worried about how the back looks.

Change to C.
Knit 2 rows.
Change to B.
Knit 2 rows.
Change to A.

MAIN PART
Row 11: Knit.
Row 12: Purl.
Cont in st st, follow the 70 rows of the chart, changing colors accordingly.
Cont in A only.
Next row: Knit.
Next row: Purl.

TOP BORDER
Change to B.
Knit 2 rows.
Change to C.
Knit 2 rows.
Change to D.
Knit 2 rows.
Change to E.
Knit 2 rows.
Change to F.
Knit 2 rows.
Bind (cast) off.

COLOR KNITTING

When knitting blocks of color, it is important to remember to twist the yarns when you start and stop using them to ensure that you don't get holes. The easy way to do this is to always pick up the new yarn from under the old yarn, so that the new color cradles the previously used one (see page 124). Don't carry all the colors across the whole blanket: the only color that continues across all rows is the ecru. Just drop the other colors, following the chart, and start using them again on the next row above. Don't worry too much about the odd gap; you can sort them out with discreet sewing on the back when the blanket is completed.

CHART

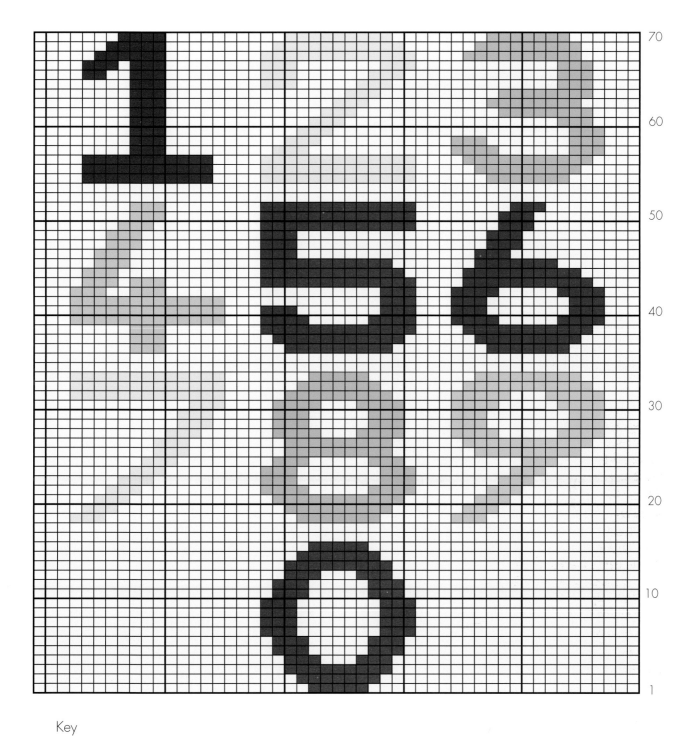

Key

A

B

C

D

E

F

CHAPTER 4

Hats & Scarves

A scarf is the classic project for a novice knitter, but it doesn't have to be a boring or frumpy scarf. There are projects in this chapter that are perfect for a complete beginner—such as the Neck Ruff (see page 86), or the College Scarf (see page 88)—and that will look chic as well as being simple to knit. If you've mastered the basics, then there are snoods and hats, lace patterns, cable knits, and color knits to try your hand at.

TWO-COLOR *Cowl*

This lovely cowl looks gorgeous, and complicated to make, but is in fact gorgeous and incredibly simple to make. As long as you can knit and purl, you can make this! The contrasting textures come from changing the side you are knitting stockinette (stocking) stitch on, so you need to be careful counting the rows, but once you've got the rhythm, you'll have no problem at all.

Yarn
Mrs Moon Plump DK (80% superfine merino wool, 20% baby alpaca) light-worsted-weight (double knitting) yarn, 1¾oz (50g), 125yd (115m) skeins
   2 skeins in Clotted Cream (A)
   2 skeins in Earl Grey (A)

Needles and equipment
1 pair of US 7 (4.5mm) straight knitting needles
Large-eyed knitter's sewing needle

Size
Circumference: 24in (60cm)
Height: 16in (41cm)

Gauge (tension)
Project gauge (tension) is 19 sts and 31 rows to 4in (10cm) over st st using US 7 (4.5mm) needles.
Standard ball band gauge (tension) is 20–22 sts and 30 rows to 4in (10cm) over st st using US 6–7 (4–4.5mm) needles.

Abbreviations
See page 126.

COWL
Using US 7 (4.5mm) needles and A, cast on 120 sts.
Row 1 (RS): Purl.
Row 2: Knit.
Row 3: Purl.
Row 4: Knit.
Change to B.
Row 5 (RS): Knit.
Row 6: Purl.
Row 7: Knit.
Row 8: Purl.
Change to A.
Row 9: Knit.
Row 10: Knit.
Row 11: Purl.
Row 12: Knit.
Rep rows 5–12, 16 more times, or as many times as you would like.
Bind (cast) off using A.

TO MAKE UP
Weave in ends (see page 124).
Right side in, fold the cowl in half. Sew the two long edges together using neat backstitch (see page 124).

CARRYING YARN FOR STRIPES
As the color changes are frequent and the edges will be hidden in the seam, I thoroughly recommend carrying the yarns up the side of the work, rather than breaking the yarn off each time you change color. If you've never done this before it simply means that you leave the color you're not working with attached to your work, then just start using it again as you need to: there are illustrated instructions on page 123. Be careful not to pull the yarn too tightly up the side of the knitting.

WORKING THE YARNOVERS

Because you are slipping the stitch with the yarn at the front of the work,
when you take the yarn to the back to knit the next two stitches together,
take it over the right-hand needle (not between the tips of the two needles)
to make a yarnover (see page 117).

BRIOCHE *Stitch Scarf*

The first thing to say about brioche stitch is that it looks much more complicated to work than it actually is. It creates a light, airy rib with a beautifully defined stitch pattern that works very well with a super-bulky (super-chunky) yarn, as the work grows quickly, but isn't heavy. You could easily follow this pattern and use the same result as a sofa throw or a bed runner. It's incredibly snuggly, and great to knit on cold evenings as it keeps you warm as you work!

Yarn

Mrs Moon Plump (80% superfine merino wool, 20% baby alpaca) super-bulky (super-chunky) yarn, 3½oz (100g), 76yd (70m) skeins
    7 skeins in Marmalade

Needles and equipment

Pair of US 17 (12mm) straight knitting needles
Large-eyed knitter's sewing needle

Size

18½ x 66in (47 x 170cm)

Gauge (tension)

Project gauge (tension) is 6 rib sts (counting both sides of the fabric) and 9 rows to 4in (10 cm) over brioche st using US 17 (12mm) needles. Standard ball band gauge (tension) is 10 sts and 10 rows to 4in (10cm) over st st using US 17 (12mm) needles.

Abbreviations

See page 126.
Note that all stitches are slipped purlwise (see page 113).

JOINING IN A NEW BALL OF YARN

One word of caution; it is quite tricky joining in a new ball of yarn anywhere other than the beginning of a row with brioche stitch, so I would really recommend being strict about that. When you do join in yarn, hold it in place for the yarnover and then after the k2tog, tie the new end to the old end, just loosely to keep it in place until it is knitted on the next row. Weave in the ends when the knitting is finished.

SCARF

Cast on 30 sts.
Row 1: *With yarn in front, sl1, yo, k1, rep from * to end of row. *45 sts*
Row 2: *With yarn in front, sl1, yo, k2tog (knitting together the yarnover made in the previous row and the next stitch), rep from * to end of row. *30 sts*
Rep row 2 until approximately 2½yd (3.25m) of yarn remains.
To bind (cast) off, p1, *k2tog, pass the first st over the second st, p1, pass the first st over the second st, rep from * until 1 st remains on the right-hand needle, fasten off.

TO MAKE UP

Weave in ends (see page 124).

CHUNKY *Cable Hat*

This fun unisex hat uses a simple cable that "grows" out of the rib stitch edging. Cables are fascinating structures and extremely simple to do; I've often been asked to run a "Learn to Knit Cables" class, but have always pointed out that it would be over in about two minutes! I've worked a contrast-color trim, but if you want the hat to be all one color, then you only need one ball of the yarn.

Yarn

Debbie Bliss Roma (100% wool, 30% alpaca) super-bulky (super-chunky) yarn, 3½oz (100g), 87yd (80m) balls
  1 ball in Ecru (A)
  1 ball in Crimson (B)

Needles and equipment

1 pair of each of US 15 (10mm) and US 17 (12mm) straight knitting needles
Cable needle (or double-pointed needle – see Working Cables, below)
Large-eyed knitter's sewing needle
4in (10cm) pom-pom maker, or two circles of card, each measuring 4in (10cm) in diameter with a central hole ¾in (2cm) in diameter

Size

One size: 12in (30cm) high (not including pom-pom), and 15½in (39cm) circumference at rim (unstretched)

Gauge (tension)

Project gauge (tension) is 9 sts and 12 rows to 4in (10cm) over st st using US 17 (12mm) needles.
Standard ball band gauge (tension) is 9 sts and 12 rows to 4in (10cm) over st st using US 17 (12mm) needles.

Abbreviations

See page 126.
C4B = cable 4 back: see page 120 for step-by-step illustrations.

HAT

Using US 15 (10mm) needles and B, cast on 44 sts.
Row 1: [K2, p2] to end.
Row 1 sets the rib patt.
Rep row 1, 7 more times.
Leaving a long end of yarn to sew up rib seam, change to A and US 17 (12mm) needles.
Row 9 (RS): Knit.
Row 10 (dec): P2tog, p2, [k1, p4] to last 5 sts, k1, p2, p2tog. *42 sts*

START CABLE PATT
Row 1 (RS): K1, [k2, p1, C4B, p1, k2] to last st, k1.
Row 2: P1, [p2, k1, p4, k1, p2] to last st, p1.
Row 3: K1, [k2, p1, k4, p1, k2] to last st, k1.
Row 4: As row 2.
These 4 rows set the cable patt.
Rep the patt 5 more times.

DECREASE FOR CROWN
Next row (dec): K1, [k2tog, p1, C4B, p1, k2tog] to last st, k1. *34 sts*
Next row: P1, [p2tog] to last st, p1. *18 sts*
Break the yarn leaving an end long enough to sew up the hat seam. Thread end into a knitter's sewing needle and thread through the remaining stitches one at a time, taking them off the needle as you go. Pull up tight.

TO MAKE UP

Turn the hat inside out and using backstitch (see page 124), neatly sew up the seam.
Using A, make a large pom-pom and sew to the top of the hat.

WORKING CABLES

A cable involves moving a group of stitches off the left-hand needle and working the next group on that needle first, followed by the ones you've moved. In the cable instruction—here, C4B—the 4 refers to the total number of stitches involved in the cable. You are generally only moving half of these stitches onto the cable needle. Don't be too concerned about having an "official" cable needle; I don't have any. Pencils come in handy (as long as they are thinner than the needle you are using), but I mostly use any double-pointed needle that happens to be lying around: much more useful in the long run.

TRIPLE-TEXTURED *Snood*

This snood is super-easy to knit; all the shaping is done using different-sized needles, so you get a beautifully fitted snood that starts wide at the shoulders and comes in snugly at the neck, without you having to worry about decreasing stitches at all. And it's knitted in the round, so there is no unsightly seaming.

It's so simple to knit in the round, and this is a great project to have a go with. If you haven't tried it before, there are step-by-step illustrated instructions on page 118.

The Alpacas and the Brushed Suri yarns used here are the same as used for the Super-Simple Textured Mitts (see page 96), and one skein of each yarn is enough for both projects.

Yarn
Blue Sky Alpacas Brushed Suri (67% baby alpaca, 22% merino, 11% bamboo) light worsted-weight (double knitting) yarn, 1¾oz (50g), 142yd (129m) balls
 1 ball in Curacao (A)
Blue Sky Alpacas Sport Weight (100% baby alpaca) sport-weight (double knitting) yarn, 1¾oz (50g), 110yd (100m) balls
 1 ball in Blue Spruce (B)
Blue Sky Alpacas Alpaca Silk (50% alpaca, 50% silk) sport-weight (double knitting) yarn, 1¾oz (50g), 146yd (133m) balls
 1 ball in Peacock (C)

Needles and equipment
US 10½ (7mm) 16in (40cm) circular needle
US 9 (5.5mm) 16in (40cm) circular needle
US 7 (4.5mm) 16in (40cm) circular needle
1 round marker
Large-eyed knitter's sewing needle

Size
Circumference at bottom 31½in (80cm)
Height 13¾in (35cm)

Gauge (tension)
Project gauge (tension) for Brushed Suri is 11 sts and 18 rows to 4in (10cm) over st st using US 10½ (7mm) needles.
Project gauge (tension) for Sport Weight is 18 sts and 26 rows to 4in (10cm) over st st using US 9 (5.5mm) needles.
Project gauge (tension) for Alpaca Silk is 22 sts and 28 rows to 4in (10cm) over st st using US 7 (4.5mm) needles.
Standard ball band gauge (tension) for Brushed Suri is 14–24 sts to 4in (10cm) over st st using US 4–11 (3.5–8mm) needles.
Standard ball band gauge (tension) for Sport Weight is 20–24 sts to 4in (10cm) over st st using US 3–5 (3.25–3.75mm) needles.
Standard ball band gauge (tension) for Alpaca Silk is 20–24 sts to 4in (10cm) over st st using US 3–5 (3.25–3.75mm) needles.

Abbreviations
See page 126.

COWL

Using US 10½ (7mm) needle and A, cast on 85 sts. Join in the round, placing a marker at the beginning of the round.
Purl 2 rounds.
Knit 20 rounds, or until work measures 4¾in (12cm) from cast-on edge.
Change to B.
Knit 13 rounds.
Change to US 9 (5.5mm) needle.
Knit 11 rounds.
Change to C.
Knit 13 rounds.
Change to US 7 (4.5mm) needles.
Knit for 9 rounds.
Change back to A.
Knit one round.
Purl 3 rounds.
Bind (cast) off loosely.

TO MAKE UP

Weave in ends (see page 124).
Carefully block as directed on the ball band before wearing (see page 112).

SPRING *Scarf*

I'm not sure whether it's my age, but I wear a scarf all year round unless it's absolutely boiling (so here in England, make that 363 days of the year!). This scarf is perfect for the spring; it's lovely and warm if needed, but also light, bright, and airy to go with the warmer weather. The stitch is really easy to pick up and looks rather lovely. If yarnovers are new to you, then turn to page 117 for illustrated step-by-step instructions on how to work them.

The picot hems can be knitted in as you go, as written out in the pattern, but if this seems a bit fiddly, then just skip doing that when you knit the rows and fold up and slipstitch the hems when you've finished all the knitting.

Yarn

Mrs Moon Plump DK (80% superfine merino wool, 20% baby alpaca) light-worsted-weight (double knitting) yarn, 1¾oz (50g), 125yd (115m) skeins
- 1 skein in Fondant Fancy (A)
- 3 skeins in Pistachio Ice Cream (B)

Needles and equipment

1 pair of US 10 (6mm) straight knitting needles
Large-eyed knitter's sewing needle

Size

57 x 13½in (145 x 34cm)

Gauge (tension)

Project gauge (tension) is 14 sts and 15 rows to 4in (10cm) over patt using US 10 (6mm) needles. Standard ball band gauge (tension) is 20–22 sts and 30 rows to 4in (10cm) over st st using US 6–7 (4–4.5mm) needles.

Abbreviations

See page 126.

SCARF

Using A, cast on 52 sts.

WORK PICOT HEM
Row 1 (WS): Purl.
Row 2: Knit.
Row 3: Purl.
Row 4 (picot row): K2, [yo, k2tog] to last 2 sts, k2.
Row 5: Purl.
Row 6: Knit.
Row 7: Purl.
Row 8 (picot hem pick-up row): Right-side out, fold up the hem along the picot row. Insert the left-hand needle into the first stitch in the cast-on row, then knit the first stitch of row 8 together with the first stitch in the cast-on row. Insert the left-hand needle into the next stitch in the cast-on row and knit it together with the next stitch of row 8. Rep from * across the row so that the hem is knitted in as the row is worked. If you prefer, simply knit row 8 and slipstitch the cast-on edge in place when the knitting is complete.

MAIN PART
Change to B.
Row 9: Purl.
Row 10: K2, [yo, k2tog] to last 2 sts, k2.

Row 11: Purl.
Row 12: K3, [yo, k2tog] to last st, k1.
Rows 9–12 set the patt.
Rep rows 9–12 until the scarf is the desired length, finishing with a row 12.
Change to B.

WORK PICOT HEM
Next row: Purl.
Next row: Knit.
Next row: Purl.
Next row: Knit.
Next row (picot row): P2, [yo, p2tog] to last 2 sts, p2.
Next row: Knit.
Next row: Purl.
Next row: Purl.

Bind (cast) off; right-side out, fold up the knitting along the picot row. Insert the left-hand needle into the first loop of B on the wrong side of the knitting, then knit the first stitch on the left-hand needle together with that loop. *Rep with the next loop of B and the next stitch on the left-hand needle. Lift the first stitch on the right-hand needle over the second stitch to bind (cast) off one stitch and knit in the hem at the same time. Rep from * across the row. If you prefer, simply bind (cast) off in the usual way and slipstitch the bound- (cast-) off edge in place when the knitting is complete.

TO MAKE UP
Weave in ends (see page 124).

SKI-BUM *Beanie*

I love a hat and I particularly love a distinctive hat: very useful in crowds or on the piste, if you are so inclined! I usually like to knit a hat in the round—mainly for reasons of laziness (no sewing up, minimal purling)—but when there is colorwork involved, it's quite good to knit flat to make sure that you aren't pulling the floats of yarn too tight, otherwise there could be a problem getting the finished hat on!
This is the absolute simplest of patterns but looks so impressive (I'm not obsessed with impressing people, but it is lovely to get compliments!). If you've not tried color stranding before, then turn to page 122 for step-by-step instructions. And if you've not worked from a chart before, then this is a good project to start with as the pattern is both written out and charted, with an explanation of how to work the chart.

Yarn
Cascade Pacific (60% acrylic, 40% superwash merino wool) worsted-weight (Aran) yarn, 3½oz (100g), 213yd (195m) skeins
  1 skein in Navy (A)
  1 skein in Blue (B)
Note that you will get several hats from this much yarn: 1¾oz (50g) balls of another worsted-weight yarn would be plenty.

Needles and equipment
1 pair of US 7 (4.5mm) straight knitting needles
1 pair of US 8 (5mm) straight knitting needles
Large-eyed knitter's sewing needle

Size
Circumference: 18in (46cm)
Height: 9¼in (23.5cm)

Gauge (tension)
Project gauge (tension) is 23 sts and 22 rows to 4in (10cm) over patt using US 8 (5mm) needles.
Standard ball band gauge (tension) is 18–20 sts to 4in (10cm) over st st using US 7–8 (4.5–5mm) needles.

Abbreviations
See page 126.

HAT

Using US 7 (4.5mm) needles and A, cast on 105 sts.

Row 1: [K1, p1] to last st, k1.
Row 2: [P1, k1] to last st, p1.
These 2 rows set rib patt.
Rep rows 1–2, 4 more times.
Change to US 8 (5mm) needles and work from chart.
Row 11 (RS): [K1A, k2B, k3A, k2B] to last st, k1A.
Row 12: [P2A, p2B, p1A, p2B, p1A] to last st, p1A.
Row 13: [K1B, k2A, k3B, k2A] to last st, k1B.
Row 14: [P2B, p2A, p1B, p2A, p1B] to last st, p1B.
Rows 11–14 set the color patt.
Rep rows 11–14, 7 more times (8 patt reps worked in total).
Rep rows 11–12 of color patt once more.

SHAPE CROWN
Row 45: [K3A, k3B, k2A] to last st, k1A.
Row 46: P1A, [p3A, p1B, p4A] to end.
Break B and cont in A.
Row 47: Knit.
Row 48: Purl.
Row 49: [K2, k2tog] to last st, k1. *79 sts*
Row 50: Purl.
Row 51: [K1, k2tog] to last st, k1. *53 sts*
Row 52: Purl.
Row 53: [K2tog] to last st, k1. *27 sts*
Row 54: P1, [p2tog] to end. *14 sts*
Row 55: [K2tog] to end. *7 sts*
Break the yarn, leaving a long enough end to sew up the seam. Thread the end onto the large-eyed sewing needle and carefully thread it through the rem 7 sts, taking them off the needle as you go.

COLLEGE *Scarf*

Vertical stripes are rather lovely, and the college look never goes out of style, but knitting vertical stripes is really rather tricky and difficult to get looking perfectly neat. So the way to get over the problem is to knit the scarf sideways, casting on along the long edge; it's really simple and very effective. You need to use a circular needle because there are so many stitches on each row that they just won't fit on a straight needle. If you've not used a circular before, this is the perfect opportunity to try one out knitting back and forth, before moving on to knitting in the round.

Yarn
Blue Sky Alpacas Worsted Hand Dyes (50% royal alpaca, 50% merino) worsted-weight (Aran) yarn, 3½oz (100g), 100yd (91m) skeins
  2 skeins in Midnight Blue (A)
  1 skein in Petunia (B)

Needles and equipment
US 10 (6mm) circular needle, at least 32in (80cm) long
Large-eyed knitter's sewing needle

Size
49 x 7in (125 x 18cm)

Gauge (tension)
Project gauge (tension) is 12 sts and 26 rows to 4in (10cm) over garter stitch using US 10 (6mm) needles.
Standard ball band gauge (tension) is 16 sts to 4in (10cm) over st st using US 9 (5.5mm) needles.

Abbreviations
See page 126.

SCARF
Using A, cast on 150 sts.
Knit 8 rows.
Change to B.
Knit 6 rows.
Change to A.
Knit 6 rows.
Rep the last 12 rows once more.
Change to B.
Knit 6 rows.
Change to A.
Knit 8 rows.
Bind (cast) off.

TO MAKE UP
Weave in ends (see page 124).

CHOOSING YARNS
Blue Sky Alpacas Worsted Hand Dyes is a really special yarn. As it's hand-dyed the color is not evenly spread, which gives the scarf a really soft, vintage look. But if you choose your colors carefully, you can use any thick worsted (Aran) or bulky (chunky) yarn.

CHUNKY *Lacy Scarf*

Proper lace knitting is a little bit outside my comfort zone; I don't have the concentration levels needed to get to the end of a very long row without making a mistake... But I do love knitted lace, so this scarf is my perfect compromise. The trickiest thing about lace knitting is keeping track of where you are in the pattern, but this lace is easy in that respect because there are two fixed points; as long as you ensure you are always purling in the same place and putting the sk2po in the same place, you can't go too far wrong.

There are lots of knitting terms that sound as though you need to complete a course to master the technique, but this isn't the case, so don't let mere words put you off. Lace knitting is just using stitches knitted together (see pages 115–17) and yarnovers (see page 117) to create holes. My two best bits of advice are; never read ahead in a pattern, and don't stress about the odd mistake; no one will ever notice, and it's useful to have something to prove that your gorgeous scarf is not store-bought.

Yarn
Purl Soho Alpaca Pure (100% super baby alpaca) worsted-weight (Aran) yarn, 3½oz (100g), 109yd (100m) skeins
  4 skeins in Pink Grapefruit

Needles and equipment
1 pair of US 10 (6mm) straight knitting needles
Large-eyed knitter's sewing needle

Size
59¾ x 11in (152 x 28cm)

Gauge (tension)
Project gauge (tension) is 17 sts and 19 rows to 4in (10cm) over lace patt using US 10 (6mm) needles.
Standard ball band gauge (tension) is 16–20 sts to 4in (10cm) over st st using US 7–8 (4.5–5mm) needles.

Abbreviations
See page 126.

SCARF

Cast on 47 sts.
Knit 3 rows.

START LACE PATT WITH GARTER ST BORDERS
Row 1 (RS): K4 [yo, k3, sk2po, k3, yo, k1] to last 3 sts, k3.
(Pattern note: this is the only row where there are no purl sts, so watch out for it as the patt repeats.)
Row 2 and all even-numbered rows: K4, [p9, k1] to last 3 sts, k3.
Row 3: K3, p1, [k1, yo, k2, sk2po, k2, yo, k1, p1] to last 3 sts, k3.
Row 5: K3, p1, [k2, yo, k1, sk2po, k1, yo, k2, p1] to last 3 sts, k3.
Row 7: K3, p1, [k3, yo, sk2po, yo, k3, p1] to last 3 sts, k3.
Row 8: As row 2.
These eight rows set the lace patt.
Rep the patt 34 more times (or until scarf is desired length).
On the final rep work rows 1–7 only.
Knit 3 rows.
Bind (cast) off.

TO MAKE UP

Weave in ends (see page 124.
Block knitting following advice on ball band (see page 112).

SWIRLY *Hat*

This lovely slouchy hat has a really interesting stitch pattern that is very simple to create by simply knitting stitches together around and around. Because of the nature of the swirl, the decrease at the top of the hat is a little more complicated than is usual. My advice is to not worry too much about the stitch count. You essentially start the next round two stitches earlier each time to keep the spiral going. As long as you are decreasing stitches at an even rate, you should be fine!

Yarn
Rowan Cocoon (80% merino wool, 20% kid mohair) bulky (chunky) yarn, 3½oz (100g), 126yd (115m) balls
    1 ball in Polar

Needles and equipment
US 10 (6mm) 16in (40cm) circular needle
Set of 4 US 10½ (7mm) double-pointed needles
US 10½ (7mm) 16in (40cm) circular needle
Large-eyed knitter's sewing needle
2 round markers

Size
10½in (27cm) across crown

Gauge (tension)
Project gauge (tension) is 16 sts and 20 rows to 4in (10cm) over patt using US 10½ (7mm) needles.
Standard ball band gauge (tension) is 14 sts and 16 rows to 4in (10cm) over st st using US 10½ (7mm) needles.

Abbreviations
See page 126.

HAT
Using US 10 (6mm) circular needle, cast on 72 sts.
Join in the round and place a marker at the start of the round.
Rounds 1–6: [P1, k1] to end.
Change to US 10½ (7mm) circular needle.
Round 7: [Yo, k2tog] to end.
Rep round 7 until hat measures 8in (20cm) from cast-on edge.

SHAPE CROWN
Change to the double-pointed needles when there are too few sts to work on the circular needle.
Next round: *K2tog, [yo, k2tog] 4 times, rep from * to last 2 sts. This point is now the beginning of the next round, so place a marker here and remove the previous marker when you get to it. *63 sts + 2 remaining*
Next round: *K3tog, [yo, k2tog] 3 times, rep from * to last 2 sts. This point is now the beginning of the next round, so place a marker here and remove the previous marker when you get to it. *49 sts + 2 remaining*
Next round: *K3tog, [yo, k2tog] twice, rep from * to last 2 sts. This point is now the beginning of the next round, so place a marker here and remove the previous marker when you get to it. *35 sts + 2 remaining*
Next round: *K3tog, yo, k2tog, rep from * to last 2 sts. This point is now the beginning of the next round, so place a marker here and remove the previous marker when you get to it. *21 sts +2 remaining*
Next round: [K3tog] 7 times. *9 sts + 2*
Cut yarn and thread through the rem sts, pull up tight and secure.

TO MAKE UP
Weave in ends (see page 124).

CHAPTER 5

For Hands & Feet

Gloves and socks might seem horribly complicated knitting projects, but for this chapter we have designed versions of both that are easy to knit, but will look amazing. The Super-Simple Textured Mitts (see page 96) are perfect for a beginner knitter—honestly they are!—and the Geometric Arm Warmers (see page 102) have no shaping to deal with, so you can concentrate on the color slipstitch pattern. To ease you in to the world of sock knitting, there is a pair of bed socks that have the simplest possible heel shaping.

SUPER-SIMPLE *Textured Mitts*

These are so quick and easy, you could knit up pairs and pairs of them in no time. They make perfect gifts, but are also perfect if you are prone to mislaying things! The mitts are also incredibly warm, which is always a bonus.

You could use any two yarns you like, but I love the different textures that the Brushed Suri and Alpacas Sport Weight make. You could use contrast colors, or toning ones as I have, but don't worry too much about whether the colors "go" exactly; these two certainly don't, but they look lovely together.

Yarn
Blue Sky Alpacas Brushed Suri (67% baby alpaca, 22% merino, 11% bamboo) light worsted-weight (double knitting) yarn, 1¾oz (50g), 142yd (129m) balls
    1 ball in Curacao (A)
Blue Sky Alpacas Sport Weight (100% baby alpaca) sport-weight (double knitting) yarn, 1¾oz (50g), 110yd (100m) balls
    1 ball in Blue Spruce (B)

Needles and equipment
1 pair of US 6 (4mm) straight knitting needles
Large-eyed knitter's sewing needle

Size
6¾in (17cm) high and 7⅛in (18cm) wide (after blocking)

Gauge (tension)
Project gauge (tension) for both yarns is 21sts and 25 rows to 4in (10cm) over st st using US 15 (10mm) needles.
Standard ball band gauge (tension) for Brushed Suri is 14–24 sts to 4in (10cm) over st st using US 4–11 (3.5–8mm) needles.
Standard ball band gauge (tension) for Sport Weight is 20–24 sts to 4in (10cm) over st st using US 3–5 (3.25–3.75mm) needles.

Abbreviations
See page 126.

MITT
Make 2
Using A, cast on 36 sts.
Knit 4 rows.
Change to B.
Row 5: Knit.
Row 6: Purl.
Row 7: Knit.
Row 8: Purl.
Change to A.
Row 9: Knit.
Row 10: Purl.
Row 11: Knit.
Row 12: Purl.
Rows 5–12 set the patt.
Rep rows 5–12, 3 more times, and then rep rows 5–8 once more.
Change to A.
Knit 4 rows.
Bind (cast) off loosely.

TO MAKE UP
Weave in ends (see page 124).
Block knitting following advice on ball band (see page 112). Fold each mitt in half, right side in, and starting at the bound- (cast-) off edge, sew up ¾in (2cm) of the side seam using B and backstitch (see page 124). Leave a gap about 3 stripes wide for your thumb (check the fit before you complete the seam), then sew up the rest of the seam.

SUPER-COZY *Bed Socks*

To be honest, I'm not really a sock person... I wear them, but I'm just not that into knitting them. People say once you've knitted one pair, you'll be hooked—but not me. However, as I spend many nights per year under canvas, I have a real need for some incredibly warm, super-soft and luxurious bed socks, and I thought, hang on... I could knit some! To keep the socks simple, I've abandoned "flaps" and "gussets" and done as easy a heel as I think is possible. These socks don't conform to normal sock-knitting rules, but they do the job perfectly well, and are really very, very lovely to wear in bed!

Yarn

Mrs Moon Plump DK (80% superfine merino wool, 20% baby alpaca) light-worsted-weight (double knitting) yarn, 1¾oz (50g), 125yd (115m) skeins
  2 skeins in Sugared Almond

Needles and equipment

Set of 5 of each of US 3 (3.25mm) and US 7 (4.5mm) double-pointed needles
2 stitch markers
Stitch holder
Large-eyed knitter's sewing needle

Size

One size: toe to heel (8in) 20cm, cuff to heel 8¼in (21cm)

Gauge (tension)

Project gauge (tension) is 24 sts and 26 rows to 4in (10cm) over main rib patt (unstretched) using US 7 (4.5mm) needles.
Standard ball band gauge (tension) is 20–22 sts and 30 rows to 4in (10cm) over st st using US 6–7 (4–4.5mm) needles.

Abbreviations

See page 126.

SOCK

Make 2
Using US 3 (3.25mm) needles, cast on 48 sts.
Divide the stitches over 4 needles (12 sts on each needle) and join in the round, placing a marker at the beginning of the round.
Round 1: [K1, p1] to end.
Round 1 sets the cuff rib patt.
Rep round 1, 4 more times.
Change to US 7 (4.5mm) needles.
Round 6: [K3, p1] to end.
Round 6 sets the rib patt for the main sock.
Cont in this rib patt until the work measures 6¼in (16cm) from the cast-on edge (about 38 rounds). You can make the sock longer here by just continuing in rib patt until it's as long as desired.

START HEEL
To begin preparing for the heel, the patt changes so that half of the stitches are st st rather than rib.
Next round: K24, [k3, p1] to end.
Rep last round 5 more times.

TURN HEEL
Slip the rib stitches onto the stitch holder and work the 24 st st stitches back and forth on 2 needles.
Row 1: Sl1, k23, turn.
Row 2: Sl1, p22, turn.
Row 3: Sl1, k21, turn.
Row 4: Sl1, p20, turn.
Row 5: Sl1, k19, turn.
Row 6: Sl1, p18, turn.
Row 7: Sl1, k17, turn.
Row 8: Sl1, p16, turn.
Now start to make longer rows again:
Row 9: K17, turn.
Row 10: P18, turn.
Row 11: K19, turn.
Row 12: P20, turn.
Row 13: K21, turn.
Row 14: P22, turn.

Row 15: K23, turn.

Row 16: P24, turn.

The heel is now turned. Put all the stitches back onto 4 needles, with 12 on each needle as before. Place a marker at the start of the st st section to mark the beginning of the round.

Next round: K24, [k3, p1] to end.

Rep last round 5 more times.

Next round: [K3, p1] to end.

Cont in rib patt for 27 rounds, or until this rib section measures 4¼in (11cm). On the last round place a second marker after 24 sts.

TOE DECREASE

Next round: [K1, ssk, k to 3 sts before marker, k2tog, k1] twice. *44 sts*

Rep this round four more times. *28 sts*

Next round: Knit.

Next round: [K1, ssk, k to 3 sts before marker, k2tog, k1] twice. *24 sts*

Slip 12 sts onto one needle and the other 12 sts onto another needle and use Kitchener stitch (see page 124) to graft these stitches together. If you really don't want to do Kitchener stitch, then just bind (cast) off all the stitches and sew the seam very neatly. Kitchener stitch means that you won't have an uncomfortable seam at the toe, but to be honest, with bed socks a seam isn't such a problem.

TO MAKE UP

Weave in ends (see page 124).

Gently press knitting following advice on ball band.

SHORT-ROW SHAPING

The heel is shaped by working shorter and shorter rows in a technique called short-row shaping. In its simplest form (as used here), you literally just turn the work at the end of each short row by swapping the needles in your hands, and continue on the next row as described. This will create small holes in your sock where the heel is shaped. As this is a bed sock, I think the holes are fine and look like a decorative detail. But if you don't want the holes, you can either use a slightly more complex method of short-row shaping and wrap and turn each time you do a short row, or you can easily sew up the holes when the knitting is complete.

SPANGLY *Legwarmers*

If there is an item of clothing that begs to be lurid, it is surely the legwarmer; this is an opportunity for really experimenting with sparkly yarns and colorful contrasts. My daughter has her eye on this pair for her dance classes, and frankly who can blame her! These legwarmers are incredibly simple to knit and can be made for a child or adult. The fact that they are knitted flat means that they are a great beginner project, but if you fancy knitting them in the round, go ahead; simply join in the round at the end of the cast on and follow the pattern as it is for the rib. Once you reach the main pattern section, follow row one only, changing the yarn every four rows.

If you substitute the wool yarn for one sold in smaller balls, a 1¾oz (50g) ball is enough for one pair of leg warmers.

Yarn

Sweet Georgia Superwash DK (100% superwash merino wool) sport-weight (double knitting) yarn, 4oz (115g), 256yd (234m) skeins
   1 skein in Ultraviolet (A)
Lana Stop Platino (100% nylon) sport-weight (light double knitting) yarn, 1¾oz (50g), 20yd (200m) balls
   1 ball in Bronze (B)

Needles and equipment

1 pair of each of US 5 and 6 (3.75 and 4mm) straight knitting needles
Large-eyed knitter's sewing needle

Size

To fit: child(adult)

FINISHED MEASUREMENTS
Length: 12¾(17½)in (32(44.5)cm) long
Circumference (unstretched): 6(9¾)in (15(25)cm)

Gauge (tension)

Project gauge (tension) for both yarns is 32 sts and 28 rows to 4in (10cm) over stripe patt (unstretched) using US 6 (4mm) needles.
Standard ball band gauge (tension) for Platino is 16 sts and 30 rows to 4in (10cm) over st st using US 8 (5mm) needles.
Standard ball band gauge (tension) for Superwash DK is 22 sts to 4in (10cm) over st st using US 6 (4mm) needles.

Abbreviations

See page 126.

LEGWARMER

Make 2

Using A and US 5 (3.75mm) needles, cast on 48(78) sts.

Row 1: [K1, p1] to end.

Row 1 sets the rib patt.

Rep the patt 7 more times.

START STRIPE PATT

Change to US 6 (4mm) needles and B.

Row 1 (RS): [P2, k4] to end.

Row 2: [P4, k2] to end.

Row 3: [P2, k4] to end.

Row 4: [P4, k2] to end.

Change to A and rep these four rows. These 8 rows form the stripe patt.

Rep the patt 8(12) more times, then rep rows 1–4 once more (both sizes).

Change to US 5 (3.75mm) needles and A.

Knit one row.

Next row: [K1, p1] to end.

Last row sets the rib patt.

Rep the patt 7 more times.

Bind (cast) off in patt.

TO MAKE UP

Weave in ends (see page 124). Right side in, fold a legwarmer in half lengthwise. Using backstitch, sew up the long seam. Rep for other legwarmer.

CARRYING YARN FOR STRIPES

As the color changes are frequent and the edges will be hidden in the seam, I thoroughly recommend carrying the yarns up the side of the work, rather than breaking the yarn off each time you change color. If you've never done this before it simply means that you leave the color you're not working with attached to your work, then just start using it again as you need to. Be careful not to pull the yarn too tightly up the side.

GEOMETRIC *Arm Warmers*

If you have never attempted color knitting before, then these striking arm warmers are a great project to start out with. They use a simple slipstitch pattern to combine the colors without the need to handle more than one color yarn at a time, or to strand the yarns across the back of the knitting. I have used yarn from small, indie dyers Fivemoons; the yarn is hand-painted, which creates light and shade within each color to fabulous effect. However, any sport-weight (double-knitting) yarn would work well, so have some fun picking shades to suit you.

Yarn
Fivemoons Hand Painted Yarn Luna Sport (100% superwash merino) sport-weight (double knitting) yarn, 1¾oz (50g), 284yd (260m) balls
- 1 ball in Sunflower (A)
- 1 ball in Anthra (B)
- 1 ball in Flannel (C)

Needles and equipment
1 pair of each of US 3 and 5 (3.25 and 3.75mm) straight knitting needles
Large-eyed knitter's sewing needle

Size
To fit: small(large)
10in (25cm) long and 7¼(8½)in (18(21.5)cm) circumference

Gauge (tension)
Project gauge (tension) is 24 sts and 41 rows to 4in (10cm) over slipstitch patt using US 5 (3.75mm) needles.
Standard ball band gauge (tension) is 24 sts and 32 rows to 4in (10cm) over st st using US 5 (3.75mm) needles.

Abbreviations
See page 126.
Note that all stitches are slipped purlwise (see page 113).

ARM WARMER
Make 2
Using A and US 3 (3.25mm) needles, cast on 44(52) sts.
Row 1: [K2, p2] to end.
Rep row 1, 6 more times.
Change to US 5 (3.75mm) needles and B.
Purl one row.

START SLIPSTITCH PATT
Row 1 (RS): Using C [k3, sl1] to end.
Row 2: Using C, [sl1, p3] to end.
Row 3: Using B, k2, [sl1, k3] to last 2 sts, sl1, k1.
Row 4: Using B, p1, [sl1, p3] to last 3 sts, sl1, p2.
Row 5: Using C, k1, [sl1, k3] to last 3 sts, sl1, k2.
Row 6: Using C, p2, [sl1, p3] to last 2 sts, sl1, p1.
Row 7: Using B, [sl1, k3] to end.

Row 8: Using B, [p3, sl1] to end.
These 8 rows form the patt.
Rep the patt 9 more times, or until arm warmer is desired length.
Knit one row in B.
Change to US 3 (3.25mm) needles and A.
Purl one row.
Next row: [K2, p2] to end.
Rep last row 6 more times.
Bind (cast) off in patt.

TO MAKE UP
Weave in ends (see page 124).
Block knitting following advice on ball band (see page 112).
Using mattress stitch (see page 125), sew the long sides of each arm warmer together, leaving a gap of 2in (5cm) just below the top rib for a thumb opening.

FINGERLESS *Mitts*

You can't have too many pairs of fingerless mitts in my opinion. In milder climes, the age of the smartphone has seen the demise of the full glove, which if you are a knitter is a bit of a blessing really—fingers can be so fiddly! These lovely mitts are knitted in the round and are super-quick to make. They are a great gift and you can get at least two pairs out of the yarn below, so you can have fun mixing up the color combinations. If you want them to be just one color, you only need one skein of yarn.

Yarn
Mrs Moon Plump DK (80% superfine merino wool, 20% baby alpaca) light-worsted-weight (double knitting) yarn, 1¾oz (50g), 125yd (115m) skeins
- 1 skein in Lemon Curd (A)
- 1 skein in Marmalade (B)
- 1 skein in Clotted Cream (C)

Needles and equipment
Set of 4 of each of US 6 (4mm) and US 7 (4.5mm) double-pointed needles
Small stitch holder (or waste yarn)
Round marker
Large-eyed knitter's sewing needle

Size
To fit average adult female hand

Gauge (tension)
Project gauge (tension) is 22 sts and 30 rows to 4in (10cm) over st st using US 6 (4mm) needles.
Standard ball band gauge (tension) is 20–22 sts and 30 rows to 4in (10cm) over st st using US 6–7 (4–4.5mm) needles.

Abbreviations
See page 126.

MITT
Make 2
Using US 6 (4mm) double-pointed needles and A, cast on 35 sts.
Divide the stitches over 3 needles (12, 12, 11 sts on each needle) and join in the round, placing a marker at the beginning of the round.

Round 1: [K3, p2] to end.
Round 1 sets the rib patt.
Rep round 1, 21 more times.
Change to B.
Round 23: Knit (this stops the color change showing on the purl stitches).
Round 24: [K3, p2] to end.
Rep round 24, 9 more times.
Change to US 7 (4.5mm) double-pointed needles.
Knit 9 rounds.

SHAPE THUMB
Round 43: K1, m1, k to last st, m1, k1. 37 sts
Round 44: K2, m1, k to last 2 sts, m1, k2. 39 sts
Round 45: K3, m1, k to last 3 sts, m1, k3. 41 sts
Round 46: K4, m1, k to last 4 sts, m1, k4. 43 sts
Change to C.
Round 47: K5, m1, k to last 5 sts, m1, k5. 45 sts
Round 48: Knit to 6 sts before marker.
Slip these 6 sts, plus the first 6 sts of the next round, onto a stitch holder or length of waste yarn.
Place marker here and using the backward loop method, cast on 4 sts.
Next round: Knit. 37 sts
Knit 6 rounds.
Next round: Ssk, k1, k2tog, knit to end. 35 sts
Change to US 6 (4mm) double-pointed needles.
Next round: P1, [k3, p2] to last 4 sts, k3, p1.
Rep the last round 4 more times.
Bind (cast) off in patt.

THUMB
Slip the 12 sts on the stitch holder onto 2 of the US 6 (4mm) double-pointed needles (6 sts on each needle). Using a 3rd needle, pick up and knit 5 stitches across the top of the thumb opening. Knit the 6 sts on the first dpn and place marker. 17 sts

Round 1: K3, p2, k2tog, k2, p2, k2tog, k2, p2. 15 sts
Next round: [K3, p2] to end.
Rep the last round twice more.
Bind (cast) off in patt.

TO MAKE UP
Weave in ends (see page 124).

CHAPTER 6
Techniques

There are projects in this book that require only the most basic knitting skills—casting on, knit stitch, and binding (casting) off—and you'll find step-by-step instructions for those techniques in this chapter. There are also illustrated instructions for other techniques used to make some of the knits, such as cables and cluster stitches. None of these skills are very hard to master, but if you haven't tried one before, then it's a good idea to knit a practice swatch before starting a project.

Holding needles

If you are new to knitting, you will need to find out which is the most comfortable way for you to hold your knitting needles. This applies to both a pair of knitting needles or a circular needle (see page 118).

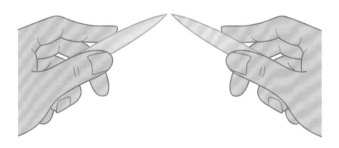

LIKE A KNIFE

Pick up one needle in each hand, as if you were holding a knife and fork—so, with your hands over the top of each needle. As you knit, you will tuck the blunt end of the right-hand needle under your arm and let go with your hand to manipulate the yarn, returning your hand to the needle to move the stitches along.

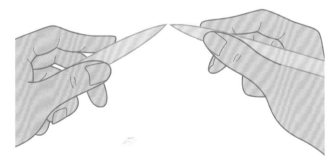

LIKE A PEN

Hold the left-hand needle like a knife, but the right-hand needle like a pen, with your thumb and forefinger holding the needle close to the point and the shaft resting in the crook of your thumb. As you knit, do not let go of the needle but simply slide your right hand forward to manipulate the yarn.

Holding yarn

The yarn you are working with needs to be tensioned and manipulated to produce an evenly knitted fabric. You can use either your right or left hand to hold and tension the yarn, depending on the way in which you are going to make the stitches (see pages 109 and 110). Depending on your natural gauge (tension), (see page 112), you will need to wind the yarn more or less tightly around your fingers. Try the methods shown here to find out which suits you best.

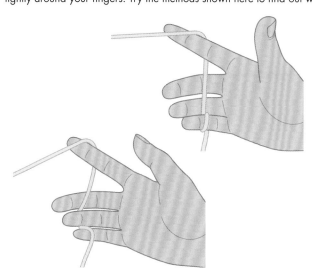

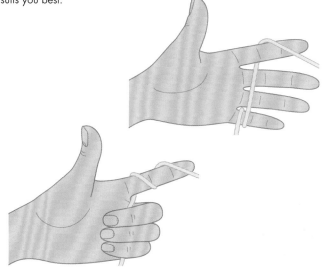

YARN IN RIGHT HAND

To knit and purl in the US/UK style (see page 109), hold the yarn in your right hand.

To hold the yarn tightly (top), wind it right around your little finger, under your ring and middle fingers, then pass it over your index finger; this finger will manipulate the yarn.

For a looser hold (bottom), catch the yarn between your little and ring fingers, pass it under your middle finger, then over your index finger.

YARN IN LEFT HAND

To knit and purl in the continental style (see page 110), hold the yarn in your left hand.

To hold the yarn tightly (top), wind it right around your little finger, under your ring and middle fingers, then pass it over your index finger; this finger will manipulate the yarn.

For a looser hold (bottom), fold your little, ring, and middle fingers over the yarn, and wind it twice around your index finger.

· ·

Making a slip knot

You will need to make a slip knot to start knitting; this knot counts as the first cast-on stitch.

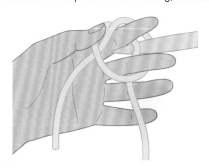

1 With the ball of yarn to the right, lay the end of the yarn on the palm of your left hand. With your right hand, wind the yarn twice round your index and middle fingers to make a loop. Make a second loop behind the first one. Slip a knitting needle in front of the first loop to pick up the second loop, as shown.

2 Slip the yarn off your fingers leaving the loop on the needle. Gently pull on both yarn ends to tighten the knot a little, then pull on the yarn leading to the ball of yarn to fully tighten the knot on the needle.

Thumb cast on

This method creates a cast-on row with a bit of stretch in it. Because you are working with the tail end (the cut end) of the yarn as well as the ball end, you need to estimate the length of yarn needed to cast on all the stitches required: allowing ¾in (2cm) per stitch is a safe amount.

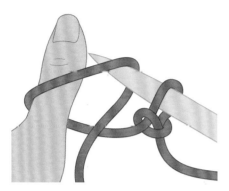

1 Measure out the required length of yarn and make a slip knot (see page 107) at that point. Hold the knitting needle in your right hand. *From front to back, wrap the tail end of the yarn around your left thumb.

2 Using your right hand, slip the point of the knitting needle under the yarn wrapped around your thumb, as shown. Wrap the ball end of the yarn around the point of the needle.

3 Pull the needle, and the yarn around it, through the loop around your thumb. Slip your left thumb out of the loop. Pull gently on the tail end of the yarn to tighten the stitch. Repeat from * until you have cast on the required number of stitches.

Backward loop cast on

This is a quick and easy method of casting on stitches; in this book it is used to cast on stitches for armholes and for the thumb of fingerless mittens. It's shown here worked after a slip knot, but the method is the same if the stitches are being cast on after an existing knitted stitch.

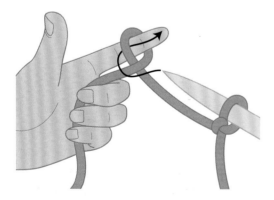

1 Hold the knitting needle in your right hand. *From front to back, wrap the working yarn around your left index finger. Slip the needle under the loop around your finger in the direction indicated by the arrow.

2 Slide your thumb out of the loop and pull the new stitch tight on the needle. Repeat from * until you have cast on the required number of stitches.

Knit stitch

There are only two stitches to master in knitting, and the knit stitch is the first one to learn. This is the method for making a stitch if you are knitting using the US/UK techniques, but you can also try the method known as Continental knitting (see page 110).

1 Hold the needle with the cast-on stitches in your left hand and the empty needle in your right hand. * From left to right, put the point of the right-hand needle into the front of the first stitch. Wrap the yarn around the point of the right-hand needle, again from left to right.

2 With the tip of the right-hand needle, pull the wrapped yarn through the stitch to form a loop. This loop is the new stitch.

3 Slip the original stitch off the left-hand needle by gently pulling the right-hand needle to the right. Repeat from * until you have knitted all the stitches on the left-hand needle. Swap the needles in your hands and you are ready to work the next row.

Purl stitch

This is the other stitch you need to learn, Again, this is the US/UK method, but you can try the Continental method (see page 110).

1 Hold the needle with the cast-on stitches in your left hand and the empty needle in your right hand. * From right to left, put the point of the right-hand needle into the front of the first stitch. Wrap the yarn around the point of the right-hand needle, again from right to left.

2 With the tip of the right-hand needle, pull the wrapped yarn through the stitch to form a loop. This loop is the new stitch.

3 Slip the original stitch off the left-hand needle by gently pulling the right-hand needle to the right. Repeat from * until you have purled all the stitches on the left-hand needle. Swap the needles in your hands and you are ready to work the next row.

Knit stitch Continental method

This is how to form a knit stitch if you are holding the yarn in your left hand and so working in the Continental style. If you are left-handed, you may find this method easier than the US/UK technique (see page 109).

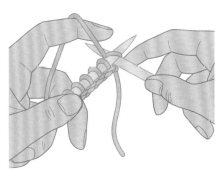

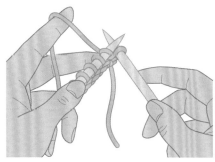

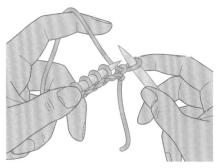

1 Hold the needle with the cast-on stitches in your left hand and the empty needle in your right hand. * From left to right, put the point of the right-hand needle into the front of the first stitch. Holding the working yarn fairly taut with your left hand at the back of the work, move the tip of the right-hand needle under the working yarn.

2 With the tip of the right-hand needle, bring the wrapped yarn through the stitch to form a loop. This loop is the new stitch.

3 Slip the original stitch off the left-hand needle by gently pulling the right-hand needle to the right. Repeat from * until you have knitted all the stitches on the left-hand needle. Swap the needles in your hands and you are ready to work the next row.

Purl stitch Continental method

Here is how a purl stitch is made when you are knitting using the Continental technique.

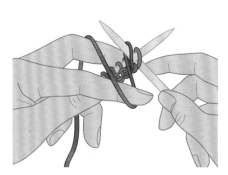

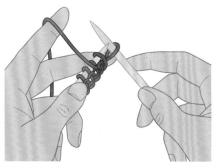

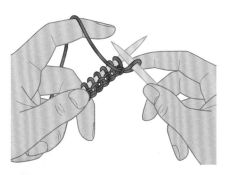

1 Hold the needle with the cast-on stitches in your left hand and the empty needle in your right hand. * From right to left, put the point of the right-hand needle into the front of the first stitch. Holding the working yarn fairly taut with your left hand at the back of the work, move the tip of the right-hand needle under the working yarn, then push your left index finger downward, as shown, to hold the yarn around the needle.

2 With the tip of the right-hand needle, pull the wrapped yarn through the stitch to form a loop. This loop is the new stitch.

3 Slip the original stitch off the left-hand needle by gently pulling the right-hand needle to the right. Repeat from * until you have purled all the stitches on the left-hand needle. Swap the needles in your hands and you are ready to work the next row.

Binding (casting) off

When you have finished a piece of knitting, you need to bind (cast) off your stitches to stop the work unraveling. You can do this on a knit or a purl row (the pattern will tell you): it's shown here on a knit row, but the principle is the same for a purl row, though all the stitches are purled rather than knitted.

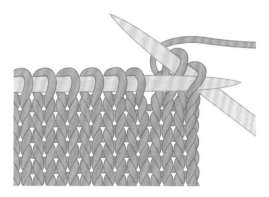

1 Knit the first two stitches in the usual way. * With the point of the left-hand needle, pick up the first stitch you knitted and lift it over the second stitch. Knit another stitch so that there are once again two stitches on the right-hand needle. Repeat from * until there is just one stitch remaining on the right-hand needle.

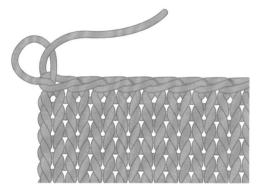

2 Break the yarn, leaving a tail of yarn long enough to weave in (see page 125). Pull the tail all the way through the last stitch. Slip the stitch off the needle and pull it tight.

Basic knitted fabrics

All knitted fabrics are based on combinations of knit and purl stitches. Some of the more complex fabrics also need stitches swapped or wrapped, but they still use the basic stitches. The fabrics shown here are all very easy to knit.

GARTER STITCH

This is the simplest of all knitted fabrics. You only need to learn knit stitch (see page 109), as every row is worked using just that stitch.

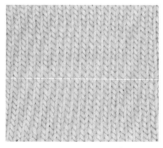

STOCKINETTE (STOCKING) STITCH

This is the most commonly used knitted fabric. To make it you work alternate rows in knit stitch and purl stitch. The "wrong" side is in fact a fabric in it's own right and is called reverse stockinette (stocking) stitch.

SINGLE RIB

The most commonly used type of rib stitch. This is made by working alternate knit and purl stitches. On the next row you purl the stitches that were knitted and vice versa to create the columns that make this very stretchy fabric.

DOUBLE RIB

This is made using the same principle as single rib, but you work two knit stitches followed by two purl stitches across each row.

Gauge (tension)

Gauge (called tension in the UK), is the word used to describe how tight or loose a piece of knitting is. This matters, because if your knitting is looser than that in the sample, then your project will be larger; and smaller if your knitting is tighter.

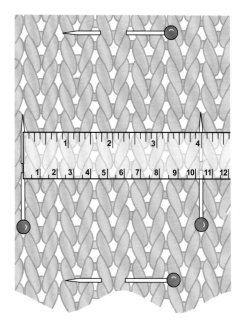

A gauge (tension) is given with each pattern to help you make your project the same size as the sample. The gauge is given as the number of stitches and rows you need to work to produce a 4-in (10-cm) square of knitting.

Using the recommended yarn and needles, cast on 8 stitches more than the gauge (tension) instruction asks for—so if you need to have 10 stitches to 4in (10cm), cast on 18 stitches. Working in the pattern as instructed, work 8 rows more than are needed. Bind (cast) off loosely.

Lay the swatch flat without stretching it. Lay a ruler across the stitches as shown, with the 2in (5cm) mark centered on the knitting, then put a pin in the knitting at the start of the ruler and at the 4in (10cm) mark: the pins should be well away from the edges of the swatch. Count the number of stitches between the pins. Repeat the process across the rows to count the number of rows to 4in (10cm).

If the number of stitches and rows you've counted is the same as the number asked for in the instructions, you have the correct gauge (tension). If you do not have the same number then you will need to change your gauge (tension).

To change gauge (tension) you need to change the size of your knitting needles. A good rule of thumb to follow is that one difference in needle size will create a difference of one stitch in the gauge (tension). You will need to use larger needles to achieve fewer stitches and smaller ones to achieve more stitches.

Blocking

If, once you have finished the piece of knitting, it doesn't look as smooth and even as you hoped it would, then blocking it can help. You can also use this process to straighten or to re-shape pieces a little if need be. The precise method of blocking you use depends on the fiber the yarn is spun from: the ball band will give you advice on that.

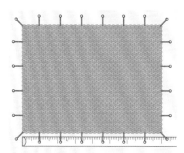

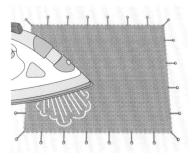

1 Lay the piece of knitting flat on an ironing board and ease it into shape. Don't pull hard and keep the knitting flat. Starting at the corners (if there are any), pin the edges of the piece to the ironing board, pushing the pins in far enough to hold the knitting firmly. Use a ruler or tape measure to check that the pinned pieces are the right size.

2 If the fiber or texture of your yarn does not respond well to heat, then use a spray bottle of cold water to completely dampen the knitting, but do note make it soaking wet. Leave the knitting to dry naturally, then unpin it.

3 If you can use heat, then set the iron to the temperature the yarn ball band recommends. Hold the iron 1in (2.5cm) above the surface of the knitting and steam it for a couple of minutes. Move the iron so that the whole surface gets steamed, but don't actually touch the knitting with the iron as this can spoil the texture and drape of the fabric and may leave shiny patches. Leave the knitting to dry naturally, then unpin it.

Slipping stitches

Slipping stitches means simply passing them from one needle to the other without knitting or purling them. They can be slipped knitwise or purlwise, but unless stated otherwise in a pattern, slip them purlwise. Stitches are slipped for some shaping techniques (see pages 114–117), and to create some stitch patterns.

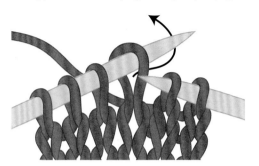

KNITWISE

From left to right, put the right-hand needle into the next stitch on the left-hand needle and slip it over onto the right-hand needle without knitting it.

PURLWISE

You can slip a stitch purlwise on a purl row or a knit row. From right to left, put the right-hand needle into the next stitch on the left-hand needle and slip it over onto the right-hand needle without purling it.

Brioche stitch

This is a lovely stitch that is used to make a wonderfully snuggly wrap (see page 74). It's easy to work using stitches that are slipped purlwise (see above). The yarn is held at the front of the work as the stitch is slipped, so just bring it between the tips of the needles to the front before you slip the stitch. If you look at the knitting pattern, you'll see that after the stitch is slipped you make a yarnover (see page 117), so having the yarn at the front means it's already in the right position to make the yarnover.

Through the back loop

You usually knit or purl stitches by putting the right-hand needle into the front of the stitch. However, sometimes a stitch needs to be twisted to create an effect or to work a technique, and to do this you knit or purl into the back of it. This is called working "through the back loop" and is abbreviated to "tbl" in a knitting pattern.

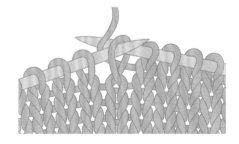

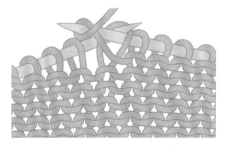

Knitting tbl

Put the right-hand needle into the back of the next stitch on the left-hand needle. Knit the stitch in the usual way (see page 109), but through the back loop.

Purling tbl

Put the right-hand needle into the next stitch on the left-hand needle. Purl the stitch in the usual way (see page 109), but through the back loop.

Increasing

This means creating extra stitches to shape your knitting. There are two main methods used in this book, both of which have variations depending on which row you are working on, and which direction the increased stitches need to slope in to create an effect.

INCREASE ON A KNIT ROW

This is usually abbreviated as "inc" in a knitting pattern. There will be a visible bar of yarn across the base of the extra stitch.

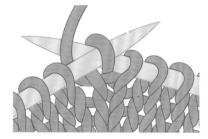

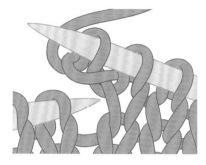

1 Knit the next stitch on the left-hand needle in the usual way (see page 109), but do not slip the original stitch off the left-hand needle.

2 Move the right-hand needle behind the left-hand needle and put it into the same stitch again, but through the back of the stitch this time. Knit the stitch through the back loop (see page 113).

3 Slip the original stitch off the left-hand needle. You have increased by one stitch.

INCREASE ON A PURL ROW

This is also usually abbreviated as "inc" when working a purl row, or "inc pwise."

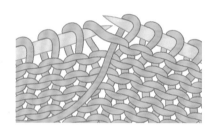

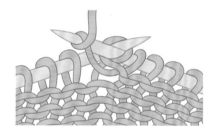

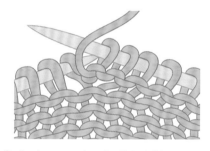

1 Purl the next stitch on the left-hand needle in the usual way (see page 109), but do not slip the original stitch off the left-hand needle.

2 Twist the right-hand needle backward to make it easier to put it into the same stitch again, but through the back of the stitch this time. Purl the stitch through the back loop (see page 113).

3 Slip the original stitch off the left-hand needle. You have increased by one stitch.

MAKE ONE LEFT ON A KNIT ROW

This method is usually abbreviated as "m1" or "m1l": if a pattern just says "m1," this is the increase it refers to. It creates an extra stitch almost invisibly.

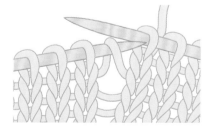

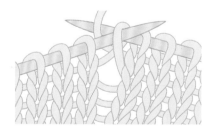

1 From the front, slip the tip of the left-hand needle under the horizontal strand of yarn running between the last stitch on the right-hand needle and the first stitch on the left-hand needle.

2 Put the right-hand needle knitwise into the back of the loop formed by the picked-up strand and knit the loop in the same way you would knit a stitch (see page 109), but through the back loop (see page 113). You have increased by one stitch.

MAKE ONE RIGHT ON A KNIT ROW

This increase will usually be abbreviated as "m1r" in a pattern. It slopes
in the opposite direction to "make one left on a knit row", opposite.

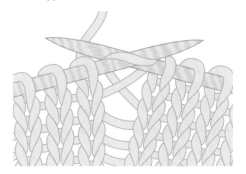

1 From the back, slip the tip of the left-hand needle under the horizontal strand of yarn running between the last stitch on the right-hand needle and the first stitch on the left-hand needle. Put the right-hand needle knitwise into the front of the loop formed by the picked-up strand, and knit it in the same way you would knit a stitch (see page 109). You have increased by one stitch.

MAKE ONE LEFT ON A PURL ROW

You can also use make one increases on a purl row, and this version
is usually abbreviated as "m1lp" or "m1p" in a knitting pattern.

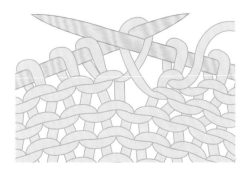

1 From the front, slip the tip of the left-hand needle under the horizontal strand of yarn running between the last stitch on the right-hand needle and the first stitch on the left-hand needle. Put the right-hand needle purlwise into the back of the loop formed by the picked-up strand and purl the loop in the same way you would purl a stitch (see page 109), but through the back loop (see page 113). You have increased by one stitch.

- -

Decreasing

This means taking away stitches to shape your knitting. The technique used will
depend on how many stitches need to be eliminated, and as with increasing
(see page 114), the methods make the stitches slope in different directions.

KNIT TWO TOGETHER

This is the simplest way of decreasing and is abbreviated to "k2tog" in a pattern.

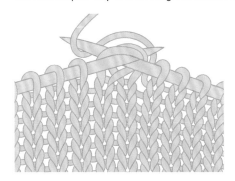

1 Put the right-hand needle knitwise through the next two stitches on the left-hand needle instead of through just one stitch, and then knit them in the usual way (see page 109) as if they were a single stitch. You have decreased by one stitch.
To knit three stitches together—abbreviated to "k3tog"—simply put the needle through three instead of two stitches and knit all three together.

Simple lace stitch

This is the stitch used to make the
Spring Scarf (see page 80). It's a
simple four-row repeat pattern, so very
easy to master, and it uses yarnovers
(see page 117) and k2tog (see left) to
make the slanting lines of eyelets.

PURL TWO TOGETHER

This is the purl row equivalent of the decrease above, and is abbreviated to "p2tog."

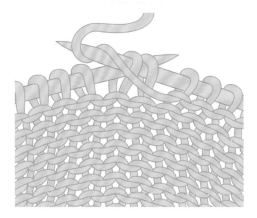

1 Put the right-hand needle purlwise through the next two stitches on the left-hand needle instead of through just one stitch, and then purl them in the usual way (see page 109) as if they were a single stitch. You have decreased by one stitch.

KNIT TWO TOGETHER THROUGH BACK LOOPS

This is a variation on k2tog that slopes in the opposite way to that decrease. It is abbreviated to "k2togtbl" in a knitting pattern.

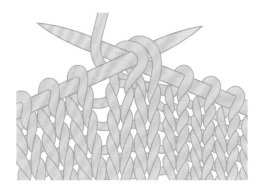

1 Put the right-hand needle through the back loops (see page 113) of the next two stitches on the left-hand needle and then knit them as if they were a single stitch. You have decreased by one stitch.

SLIP, SLIP, KNIT

This decrease requires you to slip stitches (see page 113) to twist them before knitting them together. It is abbreviated to "ssk" in a knitting pattern.

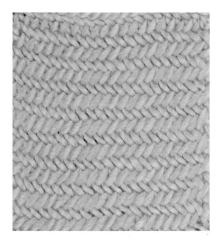

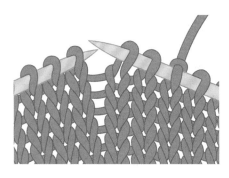

1 Slip one stitch knitwise onto the right-hand needle, and then do the same with the next stitch so two stitches have been slipped.

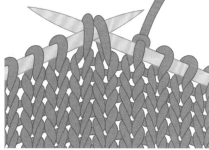

2 Put the left-hand needle from left to right through the front loops of both the slipped stitches and knit them in the usual way (see page 109). You have decreased by one stitch.

Herringbone stitch

This stitch uses ssk (see left) to twist the stitches to create a textured bed runner (see page 13). This isn't a difficult stitch to master, but it can be quite slow to work as each stitch is worked twice. This might sound a bit complicated, but work a swatch following the instructions and you'll see how simple it really is, and worth the time involved because the effect is gorgeous.

SLIP ONE, KNIT TWO TOGETHER, PASS THE SLIPPED STITCH OVER

Reduce the number of stitches by two using this decrease. The abbreviation for this varies; "sk2po" is used in this book, but "sk2togpo," and "sl1, k2tog, psso" are both commonly used as well.

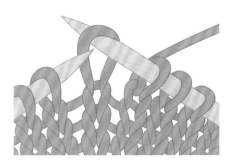

1 Slip the first stitch knitwise from the left-hand to the right-hand needle (see page 113).

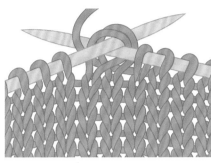

2 Knit the next two stitches on the left-hand needle together (see page 115).

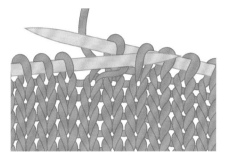

3 Finally, lift the slipped stitch over the knitted stitch and drop it off the needle. You have decreased by two stitches.

CHEVRON LACE

This is the stitch used to knit the Chunky Lacy Scarf (see page 90). The double-decrease sk2po (see above) is used to balance out the extra stitches made by pairs of yarnovers (see below). This is an eight-row pattern repeat, with all the even-numbered rows worked the same way, so it isn't hard to make this lovely lace.

Yarnovers

Making a yarnover involves winding the yarn around the right-hand needle to make an extra loop that is worked as a stitch on the next row. As well as increasing the stitch count, a yarnover makes a small eyelet. How a yarnover is made depends on the stitches either side of it; in the US all versions are called "yarnover" and are abbreviated to "yo," but in the UK each method has a separate name and abbreviation.

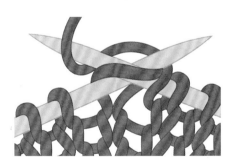

YARNOVER BETWEEN KNIT STITCHES

In the UK this is called "yarn forward" and is abbreviated to "yfwd."

1 Bring the yarn between the tips of the needles to the front. Take the yarn over the right-hand needle to the back and knit the next stitch on the left-hand needle (see page 109).

YARNOVER BETWEEN PURL STITCHES

In the UK this is called "yarn round needle" and is abbreviated to "yrn."

1 Wrap the yarn over and right around the right-hand needle. Purl the next stitch on the left-hand needle (see page 109).

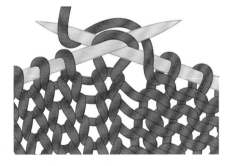

YARNOVER BETWEEN PURL AND KNIT STITCHES

In the UK this is called "yarn over needle" and is abbreviated to "yon."

1 Leaving the yarn at the front of the work, put the needle knitwise into the next stitch on the left-hand needle. Take the yarn over the right-hand needle to the back and knit the stitch (see page 109).

Picking up stitches

For some projects, you will need to pick up stitches along either the row-end edge or the cast-on/bound-(cast-) off edge of the knitting. The picked-up stitches are shown here in a contrast color for clarity.

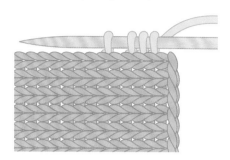

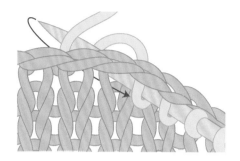

PICKING UP ALONG A ROW-END EDGE

With the right side of the knitting facing you, put a knitting needle from front to back between the first and second stitches of the first row. Wind the yarn around the needle and pull through a loop to form the new stitch. As a knitted stitch is wider than it is tall, you will need to miss out picking up a stitch from about every fourth row in order to make sure the picked-up edge lies flat and even.

PICKING UP ALONG A CAST-ON OR BOUND-(CAST-) OFF EDGE

This is worked in the same way as picking up stitches along a vertical edge, except that you will work through the cast-on stitches rather than the gaps between rows. You can pick up one stitch from every existing stitch.

Knitting in the round

You can knit seamless tubes by working round and round rather than back and forth. There are three ways of doing this, depending on how large the tube needs to be. When you work in the round you only work knit stitches (see page 109), so don't worry if you haven't mastered purl stitch (see page 109) yet.

CIRCULAR NEEDLE

These needles have short straight tips that are joined with a nylon cable. As well as the usual needle size information, the pattern will tell you what length of needle you need so that your stitches fit on it without stretching.

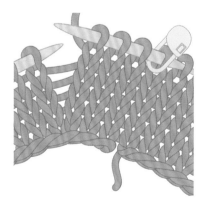

1 Cast on the number of stitches needed (see page 108); just ignore the cable connecting the two tips and cast on the stitches as if you were using two separate needles. Spread out the cast-on row along the length of the cable and make sure that it is not twisted or you will end up with a twist in the knitting.

2 Simply knit the stitches from the right-hand tip onto the left-hand tip (see page 109), sliding them around the cable as you work. The first stitch is the beginning of the round, so place a round marker on the needle to keep track of the rounds. When you get back to the marker, you have completed one round. Slip the marker onto the right-hand tip of the needle and knit the next round.

DOUBLE-POINTED NEEDLES

If you do not have enough stitches to stretch around a circular needle (see page 118), then you need to work on double-pointed needles. This is one of those knitting techniques that looks terrifying, but isn't actually that hard to do; you just ignore all the needles other than the two you are working with. Double-pointed needles—usually called "dpns"—come in sets of four or five and a pattern will tell you how many you need.

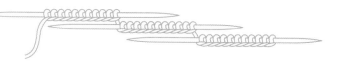

1 Divide evenly into three (if using four needles), or into four (if using five needles), the number of stitches you need to cast on. Here, a set of four needles is being used. Cast on (see page 108) to one needle one-third of the number of stitches needed, plus one extra stitch. Slip the extra stitch onto the second needle. Repeat the process, not forgetting to count the extra stitch, until the right number of stitches is cast on to each of the needles.

2 Arrange the needles in a triangle with the tips overlapping as shown here. As with circular knitting (see page 118) make sure that the cast-on edge is not twisted and place a round marker to keep track of the rounds. Pull the working tail of yarn across from the last stitch and using the free needle, knit the first stitch off the first needle (see page 109), knitting it firmly and pulling the yarn tight. Knit the rest of the stitches on the first needle, which then becomes the free one, ready to knit the stitches off the second needle. Knit the stitches off each needle in turn; when you get back to the marker, you have completed one round. Slip the marker onto the next needle and knit the next round.

I-CORDS

You knit these cords on two double-pointed needles. The number of stitches can vary, depending on how chunky you want the i-cord to be, and a firm gauge (tension) works best (see page 112).

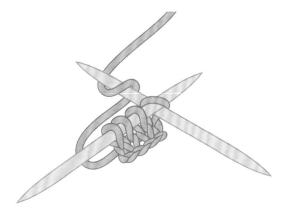

1 Cast on as many stitches as needed (see page 108): here there are four. *Slide the stitches to the right-hand end of the double-pointed needle, with the working yarn on the left of the cast-on row. Pull the yarn tightly across the back of the stitches and knit the first stitch as firmly as you can, then knit the remaining stitches (see page 109).

2 Repeat from * until the i-cord is the length you need. After the first couple of rows, it will be easy to pull the yarn neatly across the back of the stitches for an invisible join in the cord.

Cables

This is another technique that looks difficult, but really isn't. All you are doing is moving groups of stitches using a cable needle. Work a six-stitch cable as shown here: if it is a four stitch cable, then slip two stitches onto the needle and knit two, rather than three. For an eight-stitch cable, slip four stitches onto the needle and knit four; and for a ten-stitch cable, slip five stitches onto the needle and knit five.

CABLE SIX FRONT
This cable twists to the left and is abbreviated to "C6F" in a knitting pattern.

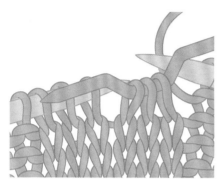

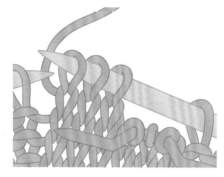

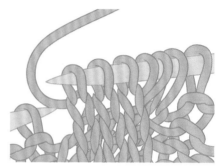

1 Work to the position of the cable. Slip the next three stitches on the left-hand needle purlwise (see page 113) onto the cable needle, then leave the cable needle in front of the work.

2 Knit the next three stitches off the left-hand needle in the usual way (see page 109).

3 Then knit the three stitches off the cable needle. The cable is completed.

CABLE SIX BACK
This cable twists to the right and is abbreviated to "C6B" in a knitting pattern.

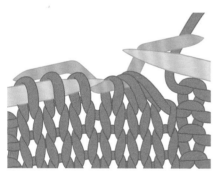

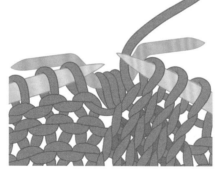

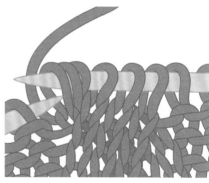

1 Work to the position of the cable. Slip the next three stitches on the left-hand needle purlwise (see page 113) onto the cable needle, then leave the cable needle at the back of the work.

2 Knit the next three stitches of the left-hand needle in the usual way (see page 109).

3 Then knit the three stitches off the cable needle. The cable is completed.

Cable pattern

This is the four-stitch back-cable used for the Chunky Cable Hat (see page 76). The Hot Water Bottle Cozy (see page 21), and the Sweetie Bolster (see page 16) are also cable projects, but they use different patterns.

Clustered stitches

This is a quick and easy way of creating a bold, chunky texture. You need a cable needle, and different numbers of stitches can be clustered together; here six are clustered.

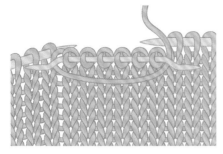 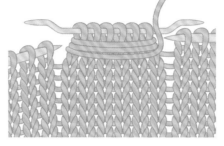 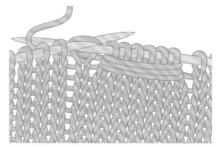

1 Knit across the stitches to be clustered (see page 109), then slip those stitches onto a cable needle (see page 113). Bring the working yarn to the front and wrap it counterclockwise around the stitches on the cable needle.

2 You can vary the number of times the yarn is wrapped around the cluster; here, there are three wraps. Finish the wrapping with the yarn at the back, and adjust the wraps to lie neatly.

3 Slip the clustered stitches back onto the right-hand needle. Knit the next stitch to hold the wraps in place, then complete the row.

Cluster stitch

This stitch pattern is used to make a textural pillow (see page 10). Don't wrap the stitches too tightly or the fabric won't be able to stretch out enough to cover the pillow pad.

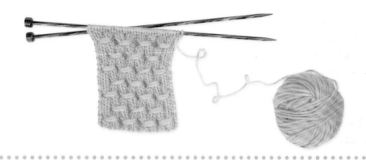

Clustered loops

These loops are worked on a wrong side row, but appear on the right side of the fabric. In the Child's Muff (see page 54), the yarn is used double, so you only need to wrap it once around your fingers to make a two-strand loop.

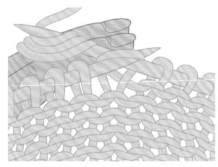 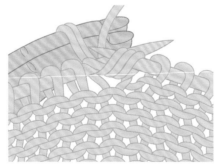 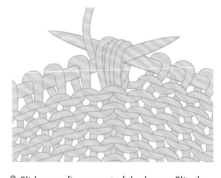

1 Purl to the position of the loops (see page 109). Take the yarn to the back (right side) of the work and put the right-hand needle knitwise into the next stitch. Hold two fingers of your left hand behind the right-hand needle. Wind the yarn over the point of the right-hand needle, then over and around your fingers as many times as you want loops, finishing with the yarn going over the needle again.

2 Pull the loops on the right-hand needle though the stitch, without allowing the stitch to drop off the left-hand needle.

3 Slide your fingers out of the loops. Slip the loops from the right-hand needle onto the left-hand needle. Knit all the loops together with the original stitch as one, knitting through the back loops (see page 113). Pull the loops firmly down on the right side.

Stranding

Often referred to as "Fair Isle," this is the method of color knitting for overall patterns. If you haven't tried it before, then it's a good idea to try it out on swatches before starting a project, as getting the gauge (tension) of the yarns right can take a bit of practice. These instructions are for the simplest method of stranding, where you work holding one yarn at a time.

CHANGING COLOR ON A KNIT ROW

It's important to swap the yarns in the right way when changing colors to keep the fabric flat and smooth.

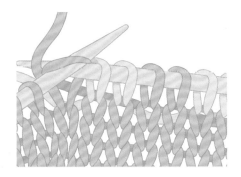

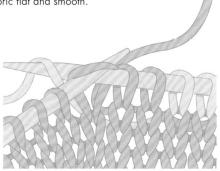

1 Knit the stitches (see page 109) in color A (brown in this example), bringing the yarn across over the strand of color B (lime in this example) to wrap around the needle.

2 At the color change, drop color A and pick up color B, bringing it across under the strand of color A to wrap around the needle. Be careful not to pull it too tight. Knit the stitches in color B. When you change back to color A, bring it across over the strand of color B.

CHANGING COLOR ON A PURL ROW

You can clearly see how the colors are swapped when working the purl rows.

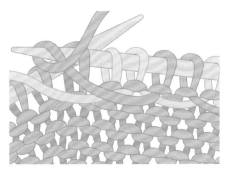

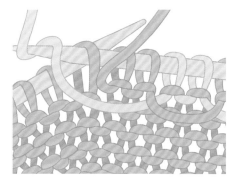

1 Purl the stitches (see page 109) in color A (brown in this example), bringing it across over the strand of color B (lime in this example) to wrap around the needle.

2 At the color change, drop color A and pick up color B, bringing it across under the strand of color A to wrap around the needle. Be careful not to pull it too tight. Purl the stitches in color B. When you change back to color A, bring it across over the strand of color B.

Stranding

These swatches show the right and the wrong sides of the chevron pattern used to make the Ski-Bum Hat (see page 83). When the yarns are swapped correctly, the back of the knitting is neat and tidy, with no loose strands that might catch and pull.

Intarsia

This method of color knitting is used for motifs rather than for overall patterns. You need a separate bobbin or ball of yarn for each area of color. It's vital to twist the yarns in the right way to link the areas of color and avoid holes appearing in the knitting, so if this is a new technique for you, do practice on a swatch before starting a project.

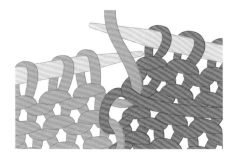

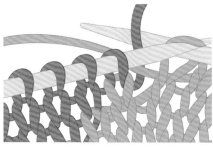

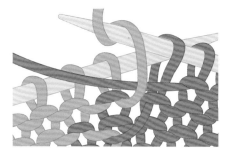

VERTICAL COLOR CHANGE

Don't rush adjusting and linking the yarns on straight vertical color changes as the stitches can become loose.

1 On a purl row (see page 109), work to the last stitch in the old color (pink in this example). Bring the new color (gray in this example) from under the old color and purl the next stitch firmly.
The same principle applies on a knit row. Work to the last stitch in the old color, then bring the new color under the old color and purl the next stitch firmly.

COLOR CHANGE ON A SLANT

Where the color change runs in a sloping line, you need to be careful that the yarns are properly linked around one another at the change.

1 On a knit row (see page 109), work to the last stitch in the old color (gray in this example). Put the left-hand needle knitwise into this stitch, then bring the new color (pink in this example) across under the old color, wrap it around the tip of the right-hand needle and knit the stitch in the new color.

2 On a purl row (see page 109), work to the last stitch in the new color (pink in this example). Put the left-hand needle purlwise into the next stitch on the left-hand needle, then bring the old color (gray in this example) up under the new color and purl the stitch in the old color.

. . . .

Carrying yarn up the side of the work

When you knit stripe patterns you do not need to join in a new color for every stripe. Instead, carry the color not in use up the side of the work until you need it again.

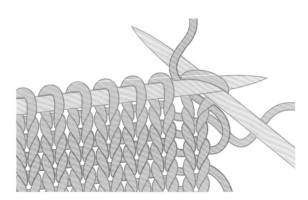

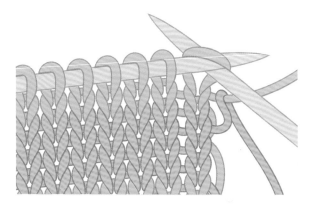

1 If the stripes change every two rows, then just bring the yarn not in use up and knit with it as needed.

2 If the stripes are wider, then you need to catch in the yarn not in use at the ends of rows to prevent long, loose strands appearing. To do this, put the right-hand needle into the first stitch of a row, lay the yarn to be carried over the working yarn, and then knit the stitch in the working yarn.

Sewing up

Different sewing stitches work best on different knitted fabrics and types of seams.
The patterns will tell you which stitch to use on a project.

WEAVING IN ENDS

Use a large-eyed knitter's sewing needle (or a tapestry needle), which has a blunt tip to weave the yarn end in and out of a few stitches. (The end is shown here in a contrast color for clarity.) Alternatively, if there is a seam to sew then you can leave a very long end and sew the seam with it.

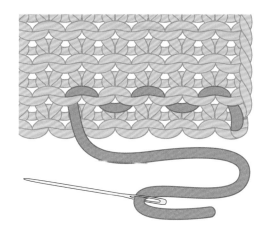

BACKSTITCH SEAM

This seam is worked on the wrong side. It is best to pin pieces together right along the length before starting sewing, and to work about one stitch in from the edge.
1 Pin the two pieces to be joined right sides together. Thread a knitter's sewing needle with a long length of yarn and secure it on the back, at the right-hand end of the seam. Bring the needle through both layers to the front, then take it back through both layers a sewn stitch-length to the left. Pull the yarn through to make the first stitch. Bring the needle to the front a sewn stitch-length to the left. *Put it in where it last came out, then bring it to the front two sewn stitch lengths to the left and pull the yarn through. Repeat from * to sew the seam.

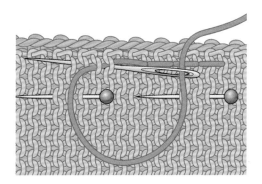

OVERSEWING

This is a quick and easy seam that is worked on wrong side, and about one stitch in from the edge.
1 Pin the two pieces to be joined right sides together. Thread a knitter's sewing needle with a long length of yarn and secure it on the back, at the right-hand end of the seam. Bring the needle through both layers to the front, *then take the needle over the top of the edges of the fabric and, from the back, go though both layers to the front again. Repeat from * to sew the seam.

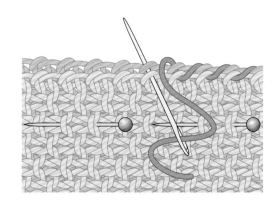

KITCHENER STITCH

This is also called grafting, and is used in this book to sew up the toe of the bedsocks so that there isn't a lumpy seam. Arrange the two needles parallel with one another.
1 Measure out the working yarn to four times the width of the knitting, cut the yarn and thread a knitter's sewing needle. From the back, bring the sewing needle through the first stitch of the lower piece and then, from the front, through the first stitch of the upper piece. Take the needle through the second stitch of the upper piece from the back, then from the front back through the first stitch of the lower piece. Bring it back to the front through the second stitch of the lower piece.
Continue in this pattern across the row, taking the sewing needle through a stitch from the front and then through the adjacent stitch on the same piece from the back. Take the needle across to the other piece of knitting and take it from the front through the stitch it last came out of, then through the back of the adjacent stitch on the same piece. Slide the knitting needles out of the knitted stitches as you join them.

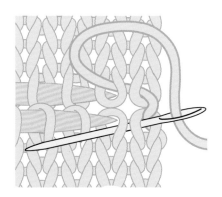

MATTRESS STITCHING ROW-END EDGES

The seam is worked from the right side and will be almost invisible.

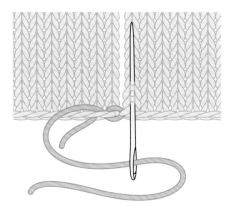

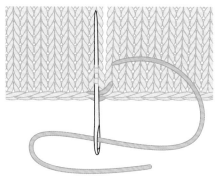

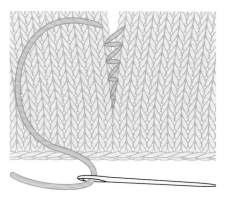

1 Lay the two edges to be joined side by side, right side up. Thread a knitter's sewing needle with a long length of yarn. From the back bring the needle up between the first and second stitches of the left-hand piece, immediately above the cast-on edge. Take it across to the right-hand piece, and from the back bring it through between the first and second stitches of that piece, immediately above the cast-on edge. Take it back to the left-hand piece and, again from the back, bring it through one row above where it first came through, between the first and second stitches. Pull the yarn through and this figure-of-eight will hold the cast-on edges level.

2 *Take the needle across to the right-hand piece and, from the front, take it under the bars of yarn between the first and second stitches on the next two rows up. Take the needle across to the left-hand piece and, from the front, take it under the bars of yarn between the first and second stitches on the next two rows up.

3 Repeat from * to sew up the seam. When you have sewn about 1in (2.5cm), gently and evenly pull the stitches tight to close the seam, and then continue.

MATTRESS STITCHING CAST ON OR BOUND (CAST) OFF EDGES

You can either gently pull the sewn stitches taut but have them visible, as shown, or you can pull them completely tight so that they disappear.

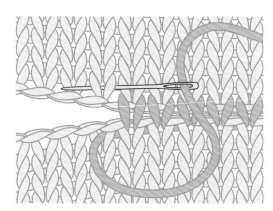

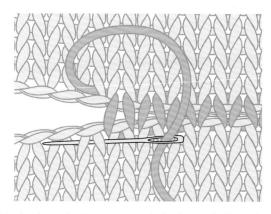

1 Right-sides up, lay the two edges to be joined side by side. Thread a knitters sewing needle with a long length of yarn.
Secure the yarn on the back of the lower knitted piece, then bring the needle up through the middle of the first whole stitch in that piece. Take the needle under both loops of the first whole stitch on the upper piece, so that it comes to the front between the first and second stitches.

2 *Go back into the lower piece and take the needle through to the back where it first came out, and then bring it back to the front in the middle of the next stitch along. Pull the yarn through. Take the needle under both loops of the next whole stitch on the upper piece. Repeat from * to sew the seam.

Abbreviations

Many knitting terms are abbreviated to keep patterns concise. These are the terms used in this book.

alt	alternate; alternatively
beg	begin(s)(ning)
C4B	cable four stitches (or number stated) back
C4F	cable four stitches (or number stated) front
cm	centimeter(s)
cont	continue
dec(s)	decrease(s)(ing)
DK	double knit
foll(s)	follow(s)(ing)
g(r)	gram
in(s)	inch; inches
inc	increase(s)(ing)
k	knit
k2tog	knit two stitches (or number stated) together
m	meters
m1	make one stitch
m1l	make one stitch left (front)
m1r	make one stitch right (back)
m1p	make one left purl
mm	millimeters
oz	ounce(es)
p	purl
pm	place marker
p2tog	purl two stitches (or number stated) together
patt(s)	pattern(s)
rem	remain(ing)
rep	repeat
RS	right side
sk2po	slip one stitch, knit two stitches together, pass slipped stitch over
sl	slip
sl2	slip 2 stitches
sm	slip marker
ssk	slip one stitch, slip one stitch, knit slipped stitches together
st st	stockinette (stocking) stitch
st(s)	stitch(es)
tbl	through back of loop
tog	together
WS	wrong side
yo	yarnover
[]	work instructions within brackets as many times as stated
*	work instructions following/between asterisks as many times as stated

Suppliers

Details of where to buy the yarns used in this book can be found through the following websites. If you can't find the exact yarns used, your local yarn store will be able to help you find a substitute.

Mrs Moon Plump: www.mrsmoon.co.uk
Big Bad Wool: www.bbwool.com
Blue Sky Alpacas: www.blueskyalpacas.com
Cascade: www.cascadeyarns.com
Debbie Bliss
  US: www.knittingfever.com
  UK: www.designeryarns.uk.com
Five Moons: www.fivemoons.co.uk
Lana Stop: www.lanasstop.com/en
Purl Soho: www.purlsoho.com
Rooster: www.roosteryarns.com
Rowan: www.knitrowan.com
Spud & Chloe: www.spudandchloe.com
SweetGeorgia: www.sweetgeorgiayarns.com

For accessories and some yarns, try the following:
UK
John Lewis: www.johnlewis.com
Hobbycraft: www.hobbycraft.co.uk
USA
Michaels: www.michaels.com
Jo-Ann Fabric and Craft Stores: www.joann.com

Index

Acknowledgments

We have had an enormous amount of fun writing our first book and have had our hands held every step of the way by the very lovely Kate Haxell, who knows everything there is to know about knitting and who has patiently and diplomatically kept us on the straight and narrow! We are immensely grateful.

Thank you to everyone at CICO Books, especially Cindy, who saw the potential, and Penny and Sally for creating such a beautiful book. Our thanks also to Marilyn Wilson for checking every single detail, and Vicky Rankin for designing the pages so beautifully.

We have to mention our Mrs Moon family: Lynn, Jodie, Kate Blue and Nathalie, who made Mrs Moon such a wonderful place to be and who have become truly great friends—and especially Jenny, who also beautifully knitted several of the samples in the book. We must also mention our Mrs Moon supporters, our many, many lovely customers, our fabulous friend Kate, Amanda for her coffee, and John, who helped us create the most amazing yarn.

When it comes to the knitty gritty, we are so grateful to our Mum, who is incredibly talented at sewing, knitting, crocheting, and everything that requires an eye for detail. Thank you Mum for teaching us when we were small... Sorry about the sewing, but hopefully we've done you proud with the knitting and crochet.

And finally, very special thanks to our families: our children Henry, Freddie, Billy, Tilly, Andrew, Florence, Ollie, and Molly, who always give the perfect reaction to any new creation and are the biggest fans you could ask for. And our gorgeous husbands, Tim and James, who have had faith, said the right things at the right times and lugged around a lot of wool...